Sugarbabies
A Holistic Guide
to Caring for Your Diabetic Pet

Randi E. Golub CVT

✧

Acknowledgements

From the time this book was just an idea casually mentioned to friends and colleagues, to its completion, I have been blessed with the support and encouragement of a great number of wonderful people.

I could not have produced this book without the technical support of the following veterinarians: Bert Boyden, DVM; Mark McConnell, BVMS, MRCVS; Sandy Smalley, DVM; Matt Fricke, DVM; Doreen Hock, DVM; Patricia Shea, DVM; Priscilla Gibson, DVM; Sarah Naidoo, DVM, MS, DACVIM; Vicki Thayer, DVM; and Jerry Boggs, DVM. Your knowledge, insight, and thoughtfulness were invaluable.

I would like to send a special thank you to Gail Schroder, DVM, Director of Shelter Medicine, Greenhill Humane Society, Eugene, OR for your friendship, for sharing your knowledge, and for never saying no to reading "just one more thing."

I would like to thank Katy Ludwig, Lyllian Breitenstein, and Judy Scher, my faithful readers, for your unique perspectives and suggestions.

To Rosie Sparks, Gus Ludwig, Gus Harschberger, Sonny Stanley, Clyde Vicale and the late Alex Golub, Easy Feiner, Gus Grabow, Thor Breitenstein, Bridey Rusby and Max Morgan, thank you for letting me into your special worlds and inspiring me to write this book.

To Mary and Herb Montgomery for generously allowing me to use excerpts from their wonderful book 'A Final Act of Caring.' I greatly appreciate being able to include this information.

iv

To Robin Gredigan and her beautiful family, Monty and Laddy, who were all very patient, adorable and photogenic! To Sweet Pea Standhardt for her modeling talents and to her Dad, Ken Standhardt, thank you for being our photographer!

A special thank you is in order for my Chip In friends who made this publication a reality.

And a most heartfelt thank you to my family, John Peterson and our precious tribe of home cats. Your love, patience, and humor has sustained me throughout this entire project.

Eugene, Oregon
August 2010

Sugarbabies disclaimer

The intent of this book is to help pet guardians and caretakers under-stand diabetes and enable them to take better care of pets with this illness. **This book is not to be used in an attempt to diagnose or treat your pet.** Diabetes is a very complicated condition, and success-ful management of diabetes depends on the good communication between pet guardian and veterinarian. If your pet shows any signs of illness, seek medical advice from your veterinarian promptly.

The author and publisher shall not be liable or responsible for any loss or damage as a result of the information contained in this book.

⟳

Introduction

The inspiration behind this book is my late cat Alex who was diagnosed with diabetes in 1999. The quest to help Alex lead a healthy and happy life was the beginning of a fascinating learning experience for me.

As a certified veterinary technician, I have helped educate clients and treat their diabetic pets for many years. When Alex was diagnosed I found myself in a unique position to more fully understand the emotions and issues concerning a diabetic pet. Initially I was scared just as you may be. I was worried that Alex would come to fear me and to run from me. Would he forgive me for sticking him with needles and making him eat a different kind of food? Actually, Alex's illness forged an even closer bond between us, and we developed an extraordinary relationship that was unlike any other I have ever had in all my years of living with cats. The lessons I learned about bravery in the face of illness serve me well to this day.

This book's goal is to explain diabetes and its treatment in simple terms, so that you can learn how best to care for your pet in a holistic context. Treating diabetes is so much more than just controlling blood glucose numbers; it means providing your pet with a healthy and balanced lifestyle. Also important is building and maintaining a successful relationship with your veterinarian as this is crucial to managing your pet's condition.

This book is written for guardians of both cats and dogs. While there are some differences in the disease process in each species, the majority of information is applicable to both species. As you read this book, you may realize that you have many questions. Your pet is very special with his or her own medical history and current condition. Some of the information in this book may not apply to your pet. You may chose to jot down questions while reading this book and discuss them with your veterinarian. The more you understand about this very complicated disease, the easier it will be for you to act in your pet's best interest.

It is my sincere hope that the knowledge I have gained will help others and will ultimately improve the lives of many loving feline and canine companions. I wish you much success, and I would love to hear your stories about caring for a diabetic pet, as well as your thoughts on this book.

Randi E. Golub, CVT
Eugene, OR
catnurseoncall@hotmail.com
www.catnurseoncall.com
August 2010

⚜

Sugarbabies: A Holistic Guide to Caring for Your Diabetic Pet

CHAPTER 1
What Is Diabetes?

What you will learn in this chapter:

- **What is diabetes**

- **How diabetes affects the body**

- **What are the different types of diabetes mellitus**

- **What are causes and/or risk factors for developing diabetes**

- **Does diet cause diabetes**

- **What are the differences between diabetes in the dog and in the cat**

Hearing your veterinarian say the word *diabetes* can be very frightening. Along with being very worried about your beloved pet, you may be wondering about the *whys*, the *hows* and the *what nexts*. There is so much to learn! But don't worry—you've come to the right place! As we travel through this book, you will learn the basic concepts, terminology, and skills to make the best decisions for your beloved friend.

What is diabetes?

Diabetes is a medical disorder that causes blood glucose (sugar) levels to be above normal. This disease affects humans as well as cats, dogs, horses, rabbits, ferrets, and even birds. It is a disease that has been recognized since the early ages. The word *diabetes* originates from the Greek word for *siphon*, as early physicians noticed how the disease made fluids flow from the body. Diabetes mellitus is caused by a decrease in the amount of insulin produced and/or a decrease in the body's ability to use the insulin that is produced. Because of this, the glucose in the blood cannot be absorbed into the cells of the body.

How diabetes mellitus affects the body

In order to function, cells in the body need energy. Glucose is the primary energy source. Glucose is a simple sugar that is the result of the digestion of carbohydrates. It circulates in the blood to be available as an energy source for cells.

Insulin is a chemical (or hormone) that is produced by cells in the pancreas. The pancreas is an organ located near the stomach. Insulin has been called the key that opens the doorway into the cells through which glucose can enter. When not enough insulin is produced or when the doorway no longer acknowledges this key, glucose cannot enter the cells and stays in the blood. The rise in blood levels of glucose pulls extra water into the urine, which causes the animal to urinate large amounts. The animal will then drink large amounts of water in an attempt to replace the water lost in the urine. While this is happening, the cells are not the getting the glucose they need. The inability of the body to use glucose as an energy source results in a starvation state that causes many animals to lose weight despite having a ravenous appetite. Because the body is not able to get the energy it needs and is therefore starving, it will break down fats and proteins to use as energy. This can cause the formation of *ketones* in the blood. (Ketones will also be found in the urine.) Ketone formation generally occurs when starvation hits a critical level or when the animal has an increased need for extra energy. This extra energy can be needed in circumstances like fighting off an infection or other disease. The formation of ketones can be the beginning of a condition called ketoacidosis, which can become life threatening. (See chapter 13.)

The Four Types of Diabetes Mellitus

In human medicine, there are four well-defined types of diabetes mellitus; Type 1 and type 2 diabetes are the most common. Current thinking now shows that these terms may not be as accurate when describing diabetes mellitus (DM) in the cat and dog. The following information is based on classifications in human medicine.

Type 1 is insulin-dependent diabetes mellitus (IDDM). The body produces little to no insulin. Treating this form of diabetes mellitus requires lifelong insulin injections.

Type 2 is noninsulin-dependent diabetes mellitus (NIDDM). In type 2 diabetes not enough insulin is produced in the body and/or its action is suppressed for different reasons. Obesity plays a big part in this type of diabetes. This type of DM can be improved with diet and/or oral medications. Insulin injections may or may not be required. Most cats will be type 2 diabetics. Early intervention of insulin therapy, in even suspected type 2 diabetic cats, may help many cats to be nondiabetic in the future. This may result from protecting the pancreatic islet cells from permanent death due to chronic levels of high blood sugar.

In cats especially, the line between type 1 and type 2 maybe be very indistinct. The disease process can be complicated by many factors that may cause a cat to go from a type 2 diabetic to a type 1 diabetic. And while it is a complicated process, many veterinarians agree that if the blood sugar is well controlled with insulin injections, many of these cats may have the toxic effects on the insulin producing cells reversed. Once these effects are reversed and the causative factors (such as obesity) are addressed, the cells may be able to produce insulin again. Everyone is happy when this happens...and it does happen!

Type 3 is impaired glucose tolerance (IGT). In cats and dogs, this form of DM can be hormonally induced. Some hormones (and medications) such as epinephrine, cortisol, glucagon, and progesterone can interfere with insulin action and cause glucose intolerance. This intolerance leads to diabetes.

Some veterinarians will include characteristics of type 4 DM with type 3. Others will classify it as follows:

Type 4 is secondary diabetes mellitus. This happens when elevated blood sugar levels develop as the result of another medical condition. In dogs and cats, this can result from chronic pancreatitis, trauma, or surgical removal of the pancreas. Diabetes can also result from other hormonal disturbances, such as Cushing's disease (hypoadrenocorticism) in dogs. In humans, gestational diabetes is included in type 4 diabetes.

Causes and/or risk factors for diabetes mellitus

Risk factors are qualities and/or conditions that cause a higher likelihood of occurrence. In the cat and dog, they include:

- Age – Older animals are more at risk.

- Breed – Some dog breeds are more commonly affected.

- Sex – Males cats are at slighter higher risk of developing diabetes while female dogs may be at a higher risk.

- Obesity – A large percentage of body fat causes resistance to insulin function. There is currently debate over how large a role obesity plays in canine diabetes, but it is well recognized in cats. An obese cat is many times more likely to become diabetic.

꜊ Disease – Certain diseases may cause diabetes or make it worse.

꜊ Medications and hormones – Some medications are known to interfere with the action of insulin and may cause diabetes.

꜊ Genetic predisposition – Diabetes running in some family lines may lead to higher risk.

꜊ Reproductive status – Unspayed female cats and dogs produce progesterone, a hormone that helps cause insulin resistance. (If unspayed, it is recommended that any diabetic cat or dog be spayed to prevent fluctuations in hormones.)

Diet as a cause of diabetes

There are many recognized causes of diabetes, including diet. And much debate over the role diet plays in the development of the disease and many different theories on this. One theory is that cats as carnivores are not able to process the large amount of carbohydrates that are typically found in dry food diets. Cats can't use large amounts of carbs, so they get stored as body fat. The resulting obesity causes the body's sensitivity to insulin to decrease. Very simply put, the pancreas then works over time producing more insulin. Higher and higher blood glucose (sugar) levels cause dysfunction of certain insulin producing cells. Eventually the cat becomes diabetic from too little insulin in the face of too much sugar. Although some studies have proved otherwise, many veterinarians believe dry food diets are a contributing cause of diabetes and the debate continues!

Diabetes in the Cat

In cats, diabetes tends to occur more frequently in middle age, roughly eight- to ten-years-old, although they may also be diagnosed at a younger or older age. Overweight cats are at a much higher risk. Diabetes is slightly more common in neutered male cats. Purebred cats and domestic short-haired cats (DSH) are equally affected, although it has been reported in Australia that Burmese cats may be more likely to develop diabetes. The important conditions associated with diabetes in the cat are obesity, pancreatitis, and as a result of specific drugs that have been given.

Many experts feel that type 2 diabetes mellitus is more common in the cat. These are cats that fail to respond to oral medications and diet alone to bring down the levels of blood glucose.

Type 2 or noninsulin dependent diabetes mellitus is more often recognized in the cat than in the dog. With oral medications and specific diets, this condition can be managed successfully in some cats; however, as the disease progresses, cats will often need insulin injections.

Because there is no reliable test to differentiate between the different types of diabetes, often a veterinarian will choose an initial treatment based on the clinical signs, presence or absence of ketoacidosis, (see chapter 13), the cat's general health, and the guardian's preference.

A few cats get transient diabetes mellitus, wherein the signs resolve after starting treatment and insulin can be discontinued. Sometimes these cats can revert back to the diabetic state if drugs or disease stress the pancreatic insulin-secreting cells.

Diabetes in the Dog

In dogs, risk factors include the fact that some breeds are more commonly affected. These breeds include Standard and Miniature Schnauzers, Miniature and Toy Poodles, Samoyeds, Lhasa Apsos, some terrier breeds (Australian, Fox, Cairn, and Yorkshire), and Pugs. Golden Retrievers and Keeshonds may be more susceptible to juvenile diabetes mellitus. (This occurs in dogs less than one-year-old and is uncommon.)

Female dogs are twice as likely as males to develop diabetes. The most common age range at diagnosis is seven to nine years.

There are several conditions that may cause diabetes mellitus in dogs. The most common causes of diabetes in the dog are acute pancreatitis and ***immune-mediated*** destruction of the pancreas, ***insulin-antagonistic*** diseases, and drugs. Type 1 diabetes is the most common form of diabetes in the dog.

Transient diabetes is very uncommon in the dog. It usually occurs in dogs that are treated with drugs such as ***glucocorticoids*** or in the early stages of other disorders.

By having a basic knowledge of DM and its effects on your pet's body, you will more fully understand your pet's condition. Although this can be a complicated disease, with this knowledge you can now begin to help restore your pet's health. In the following chapters, we will discuss how to go about doing this. Now, let's get started!

∾⚮∾

CHAPTER 2
The Signs of Diabetes

What you will learn in this chapter:

- How to recognize common signs of illness in older pets

- How to recognize the specific signs of diabetes

- What are signs of diabetes in cats

- What are signs of diabetes in dogs

- **What is the connection between diabetes and urinary infections**

- How to recognize changes in your pet's habits

With advances in veterinary medicine, the average dog lives about twelve years and the average cat fourteen years. Most veterinarians consider a cat or dog over eight-years-old to be senior. In some large breed dogs, this age may be younger. Just as with humans, animals begin to show outward signs of aging and illness as they get older. Some signs may be very obvious, while others are very subtle.

Common signs of illness, including diabetes

Diabetes is a disease that can cause illness in older pets. Unfortunately, there are several other diseases with similar signs. In the cat, hyperthyroidism and chronic renal failure are two very common diseases of older cats with similar signs such as increased drinking and urinating. Weight loss may also be present.

In the dog, chronic renal failure and some cancers may present signs similar to diabetes.

Chapter 3 discusses the importance of blood work and observation of signs in making the diagnosis of diabetes as well as ruling out **concurrent** illnesses.

Specific Signs of Diabetes

Although the signs may be similar in other diseases, the specific signs of diabetes include increased drinking, urination, appetite, and weight loss. As a result of the ongoing disease process, lethargy, dehydration, vomiting, diarrhea, respiratory problems, weakness, collapse, and coma may occur. These are signs of diabetic ketoacidosis, (DKA) a condition that requires emergency treatment. DKA will be more fully discussed in chapter 13.

Signs of Diabetes in Cats

The most common indicators of diabetes in cats reported by their guardians are excessive drinking and increased urination, as well as weight loss. They often report that the litter box seems much wetter even if they cannot say more water is being drunk. Especially in cats, a ravenous appetite may be noticed. Weight loss in long-haired cats is often not noticeable. A cat may lose a significant amount of weight before it is obvious.

Some guardians notice that their cats may have difficulty in or a reluctance to jump. (See chapter 15.) They may also be noticed walking lower on their back feet in a plantigrade stance. It appears as if they are walking on the soles of their feet (think of a bear walking) as opposed to the correct way of walking, which is on their toes. This is also called peripheral neuropathy, a condition that is directly related to the severity as well as the duration of hyperglycemia (increased levels of glucose in the blood). This condition is much less common in dogs. Dr. William Fortney of Kansas State University has observed a condition described as *frosty paws*, which occurs when the combination of neuropathy and sticky cat litter (due to excess sugar in the urine) cause the cat's paws to appear frosted with litter.

Also noted in diabetic cats is decreased interaction with family, as well as matted, greasy, and/or flaky hair.

Signs of Diabetes in Dogs

Similar signs are reported in dogs, along with a sudden loss of house-breaking, resulting in the dog urinating in the house. The loss of housebreaking in dogs is not necessarily a behavioral problem but due to the large amounts of urine the dog is producing; the increased volume means they are less likely to be able to hold it until they can go outside to urinate.

As with cats, long-haired or fluffy dogs may lose a significant amount of weight before it becomes obvious.

Dogs may become blind relatively quickly. Excessive levels of glucose also filter into the lens of the eye resulting in **cataracts,** which may come on suddenly. (See chapter 15).

Diabetes and Urinary Tract Infections

Another common sign of diabetes is recurring urinary tract infections (**UTI**). The excess sugar in the urine makes the urinary bladder an excellent environment for bacteria to flourish. Occasionally, urinalysis performed because of a urinary tract infection leads to the diagnosis of diabetes when the presence of sugar in the urine is revealed. The guardian may not have even suspected diabetes as the cause of illness.

Some diabetic animals may even have *silent* urinary tract infections. Because they are urinating so much and have a decreased ability to fight off infection, many diabetic animals will have urinary tract infections but show no clinical signs. These infections may not even be picked up on routine urinalysis as the bacteria may be washed out in the large amount of urine. Pus, a product of the infection-fighting process that may be found in infected urine, may not be present because of the pet's decreased immune response to infection. For these reasons, a urine culture should be done on all newly diagnosed diabetic pets and those that are not well controlled.

Changes in Habits and in the Household

It is much easier in the single-pet home to notice slight changes in an animal's habits. You may notice the water bowl needs to be refilled more often or the amount of food consumed is noticeably more or less. Changes in urination habits may be seen in a litter box that is much wetter than before or a dog requesting more trips outside. In the multiple-pet home, it is harder to monitor an animal's daily habits and to notice early changes. Cats that are indoor/outdoor and do not use one litter box consistently or dogs that use the doggie door may have increased urination without it being noticed. Cats and dogs that go outside and drink out of ponds and pools of water may be drinking larger amounts of water without that being noticed as well. Suggestions for monitoring your diabetic pet will be discussed more fully in chapter 8.

If your pet has already been diagnosed with diabetes, you may be familiar with these signs. You may have noticed very subtle or very dramatic changes. Often it is just an intuitive feeling that they are "just not themselves lately." In the next chapter, we will learn how your veterinarian will use these signs to help diagnose diabetes.

Any of these signs may be indicators of a medical problem, and you should discuss them as soon as possible with your veterinarian.

CHAPTER 3
Diagnosing Diabetes

What you will learn in this chapter:

- What are basic veterinary care recommendations

- What is included in your pet's medical history

- What is baseline information

- What are commonly ordered laboratory tests

- When will your veterinarian recommend testing your pet for diabetes

- What tests are used to diagnose diabetes

- How diabetes can be "accidentally" found

- How is the diagnosis of diabetes confirmed

It is recommended that you have a veterinarian examine your pet cats and dogs at least once a year (or as soon as possible when health issues arise). At that time, your veterinarian will take a complete medical history and ask you many questions about your pet's lifestyle and habits. Your veterinarian may also discuss behavioral issues with you. Next, they will do a complete physical exam that includes looking at external things such as the ears, eyes, teeth, skin, and general appearance of your pet. They will evaluate the heart, lungs, and abdomen, and also feel for any swellings, lumps, or other abnormalities.

The history taking and physical exam may be fairly brief, or in the case of a young or elderly animal, more lengthy. This is the best time to ask questions and address issues that you have noticed in your pet.

Your Pet's Medical History Includes:

- Date of examination

- Signalment (Guardian and pet identification)

- Presenting complaint (reason for the exam)

- Past medical history

- History of present illness (or is this a yearly or well-animal exam?)

- Current health status

- Systems review - Your veterinarian will ask questions about major body systems, such as the presence of any coughing or sneezing, vomiting or diarrhea)

- Pet's family history (history of parents and/or littermates)

- Vaccination and deworming history

- Has your kitten or cat been tested for FeLV/FIV?

- Has your dog or cat been tested for heartworm disease?

- Has your pet had recent blood work or a fecal test?

- Travel history (Is your pet from another part of the country and do you travel with your pet?)

- Diet history (What do you feed your pet?)

Environmental history (Indoor only, outdoor only, or indoor/outdoor?)

There are times when certain signs or behaviors that you report may prompt your veterinarian to suggest running diagnostic tests such as **blood work, urinalysis** (complete analysis of the urine) or **fecal** (feces) tests.

When to Test for Diabetes

As part of establishing a good medical history on your pet, your veterinarian will ask about your pet's daily habits, including its eating and drinking patterns. Perhaps you have told your veterinarian that your older cat seems to be drinking more than normal or your dog seems to have forgotten its house training. Because excessive drinking and urinating are classic signs of diabetes (as well as other illnesses), your veterinarian will want to run blood work to help make the correct diagnosis of what is going on with your pet. Your long-haired cat may look the same to you but weighs three pounds less than last year. Because weight loss is another common symptom, your veterinarian will want to run blood work to help find out the cause.

Doing blood work and a urinalysis are also recommended for all cats and dogs over eight-years-old (or earlier if a large breed dog) even if a specific problem is not noted. Blood work is routinely run to establish **baseline information**. Baseline information is your pet's health status when your pet is healthy. It will also be used at a later date to see how your pet is responding to treatment or the progression of any problems. It is basically a starting point from which to monitor your pet's health.

Commonly Requested Tests

Commonly requested blood tests are **serum** (the liquid portion of the blood, without cells) **chemistry tests** (chem), and **complete blood counts** (CBC.) Serum chemistry tests check the status of organ function, **electrolytes**, blood glucose levels, as well as checking for other conditions and diseases. Complete blood counts check the numbers, sizes, and types of red and white blood cells that give information on hydration status, anemia, infection, and the immune system's efficiency. Whole blood also includes **platelets**. Numbers of platelets are counted to assess the blood's ability to clot.

Another blood test may be done to check thyroid function, especially in older animals. In their later years, cats are prone to **hyperthyroidism**, while dogs are prone to **hypothyroidism**. To assure as accurate a test as possible, follow your veterinarian's instructions about whether to have your pet fast before testing.

If this has not already been done, cats should be tested for **feline leukemia virus** (FeLV) and **feline immunodeficiency virus** (FIV). Dogs and cats at high risk because of their location should be tested for heartworm disease.

Urine Testing

As part of establishing your pet's current health condition, your veterinarian may also request that a urinalysis be run. A complete urinalysis is composed of two parts. This includes using a urine reagent strip that determines the presence of glucose, protein, red and white blood cells, **bilirubin**, and **ketones**. The presence of ketones helps to identify a condition called **diabetic ketoacidosis** or DKA. (See chapter 13.) Also tested are the **pH levels** and **specific gravity** (concentration) of the urine. Microscopic examination of the urine sample looks for **urinary crystals**, cells, bacteria, **casts,** and other indicators of a problem. (Although current thinking is that a certain number of crystals may be a normal finding.)

A urine **culture** and **sensitivity** can reveal additional information about your pet's health. A urine culture is a method used to grow and identify bacteria that may be causing a urinary tract infection. The sensitivity test enables veterinarians to prescribe the correct antibiotic to treat the infection.

There are several methods for collecting urine. If the test is only for glucose and ketones, a sterile sample is not needed. Methods for collecting urine include:

Cystocentesis – This method is used when a sterile urine sample is needed and is done in the hospital. Both cats and dogs usually tolerate this procedure well from a lying-down position, although some dogs may be more comfortable standing up. The doctor or technician will first palpate to feel the urinary bladder. The bladder when full feels like a small water balloon. They will next insert a sterile needle into the bladder through the abdominal wall and withdraw urine. If you know that your pet is going to have this procedure done, putting extra water in the pet's food or offering broth can help ensure the pet arrives at the hospital with a full bladder. When taking your cat into the hospital for this procedure, do not put a towel or cloth in the carrier. Your cat may be less inclined to urinate in the carrier if there is nothing soft in it. One veterinarian has observed that cats seem to urinate after eating. She recommends that her patients not feed their cats if they're scheduled for an early morning urine sample. With a diabetic cat this could be a concern, so check with your veterinarian before withholding your pet's food.

Free catch – This method is used when a urine sample need not be sterile or when other methods of obtaining urine are unsuccessful. The urine is caught in a cup or flat container while the animal is urinating or obtained from a clean litter box. This method is used at home or in the hospital. (See chapter 11.)

Fecal Testing

Fecal tests also help to establish baseline information. For good health, your pet needs to be free from internal parasites, as well as bacterial overgrowth.

Because disease is not always apparent as animals can be very good at masking signs and/or it can be hard to monitor their signs, these tests are important parts of establishing your pets complete health profile.

The Importance of Blood Work in Ruling out Concurrent Diseases

Because the signs of diabetes can be similar to other diseases, doing blood work can rule out, or establish the presence of, other medical conditions. Some animals have concurrent conditions, which means they have several different conditions affecting them at one time. By identifying them and planning an appropriate course of treatment, your veterinarian will be more able to treat a potentially complicated situation.

Making the Diagnosis of Diabetes

- The diagnosis of diabetes is made when the following occurs:

- Persistent hyperglycemia (high levels of glucose in the bloodstream)

- Classic signs (Weight loss, increased appetite, increased water consumption, and increased urination)

- Presence of glucose in the urine (glucosuria)

It may not be that simple in some cases though, as veterinarians report nondiabetic pets that have high blood glucose readings as well as urine glucose that is induced by stress. In cats, stress hypergycemia, is very common. See below.

In the United States, your pet's blood glucose (BG) level will be reported as being as ___ mg/dL or (milligrams per deciliter). In countries such as England, Canada, and Australia, BG is reported as ___ mmol/L (millimoles per liter). The decimal mg/dL is always much higher than the metric mmo/L. **Glucometers** in the United States are programmed in mg/dL, although you should always double check this.

The normal level of BG in cats and dogs is approximately 80-130 mg/dl or 3.3 – 7.8 mmol/L. Following a meal or excitement, the levels may rise to 250-300 mg/dl. When excitement, stress, or handling causes this elevation of blood glucose it is called stress-induced hypergly-cemia. This is much more common in cats. The start of a cat's high blood glucose level may begin at the sight of the cat carrier, continue through the car ride, continue to rise when sitting next to a barking dog in the veterinarian's office, and therefore be very high at the actual time of the blood draw! These factors are considered when an excited or stressed animal has blood drawn in a veterinary office. But only diabetes will cause the blood glucose level to rise significantly above 400 mg/dl. The usual range for diabetic dogs and cats that are unregulated is usually between 400-600 mg/dl, but, in cats, the blood glucose may rise as high as 800 mg/dl. Your veterinarian will establish the diagnosis of diabetes based on persistently high levels of blood glucose as well as other factors.

While stress (especially in cats) can cause BG levels to go up to 300-400 mg/dl, ketones will not be present.

In chapter 8, you will learn what specific blood tests your veterinarian will use when monitoring your diabetic pet. These tests, Fructosamine and Glycosylated Hemoglobin, may also be used to diagnose a diabetic pet, as neither test is affected by stress at the time of the blood draw.

Glucosuria (glucose in the urine) often confirms the diagnosis of dia-betes, although, as noted above, stress can cause glucose to be found in the urine. It may not be that simple to diagnose in some cases, as veterinarians do report nondiabetic pets with high BG readings and urine glucose because of stress. If in doubt, your veterinarian may send you with a home urine collection kit or advise you on how to monitor your pet's urine at home. (See chapter 11.)

An Accidental Diagnosis of Diabetes

Sometimes diabetes is discovered by accident. Some common side effects of diabetes include recurrent urinary tract infections (UTI) and inappropriate urination. (Urinary tract infections are discussed in chapter 2). Inappropriate urination is when your pet urinates any-where other than an acceptable place like the litter box or outside the house. Cats will stop using the litter box and urinate in places like the laundry basket, bedding, bathmats, carpets, or even in house plants. (Or they may continue to use the litter box, as well as use other places.) Dogs may forget their housebreaking habits and just leave puddles on the floor. The first step in making the distinction between a behavioral or medical cause for inappropriate urination is doing a urinalysis.

Discussing the Test Results with Your Veterinarian

When all of the test results are in, your veterinarian will consult with you on the findings and discuss a plan of action. If the diagnosis of diabetes has been made, your veterinarian will decide on a treatment plan that may or may not include insulin injections.

You may feel overwhelmed by the amount of information that your veterinarian offers. While the diagnosis of diabetes (alone or in combination with other conditions) can initially be scary, as you learn about the disease, you will have more confidence in making decisions concerning your pet's welfare.

In the next chapter we will discuss the emotions and decisions you may encounter. By having the information you need and being honest about your emotional and financial resources, you will be able to make the best decisions for your beloved friend.

♆

CHAPTER 4
Starting Treatment

What you will learn in this chapter:

- What are some of the emotions involved when learning that your pet is diabetic

- What are the considerations in determining whether to treat your pet

- How to treat the difficult diabetic patient

- What are the costs involved in treatment

- What do I do if I have reservations about giving injections

- What are possible changes to you and your pet's lifestyle

- How to deal with your emotions during your pet's treatment

Finding out your pet is diabetic

You may have suspected that your pet was ill, or the diagnosis of diabetes may have come as a surprise. In any case, you may experience many emotions surrounding this news. The news can be especially sad or frightening because of the bond we have with our pets.

The human-animal bond has been given much thought and attention throughout the years, especially in today's society. Many of us regard our pets as more than just "the cat" or "the dog." They are our confidantes, best friends, family members, or even the children we never had. Whatever our attachment, we feel a great responsibility to them. It scares us to learn that they are ill, especially with an illness that may possibly shorten their lives. In most cases we just want to believe they will always be with us, fearing the day when we have to say good-bye. As scary as the news may be, remember, in most cases diabetes is a treatable condition. Although it is usually the older animal that is diagnosed, animals can live out their lifespan with good, consistent medical care and attention paid to diet and exercise needs. Age alone is not a reason to euthanize a pet nor is diabetes.

The word *diabetes* has many associations. Many people are already familiar with diabetes because they have diabetic friends, family members, or pets, or they may even be diabetic themselves. Depending on a person's knowledge and/or experience with diabetes, there will be different associations with the disease. It is essential that you become familiar with the disease itself, and your pet's unique medical condition. It is also important to be aware that human diabetics suffer serious problems that animals do not; this is attributable to the fact that most human diabetes-related complications can take ten to twenty years to develop. Animal diabetes can be easier to treat than human diabetes in that we generally have more control over an animal patient's diet and lifestyle—something that is not usually the case with humans. These are factors that help greatly in the regulation of the disease.

Gathering all your facts when making a decision

As discussed in chapter 3, it is very important to get the whole picture of your pet's condition when the diagnosis of diabetes is made. Only when you have the complete picture can you make the very best decision for both you and your pet. If you have an easy-to-handle pet with no health issues other than diabetes, the decision to treat may be an easy one. But for a difficult-to-handle pet with concurrent health issues, the decision to treat may be complicated. Successful management of diabetes begins with a good working relationship with your veterinarian. Throughout the treatment process you will have many questions, so good communication is essential!

Treating the difficult-to-handle pet

Some pets may be labeled as fractious or AWC (approach with caution) in the hospital. They may be challenging to handle even at home. Although much thought must be given to treating these animals, many people have found a way to work with their pet's difficult behavior. A lot of this behavior is caused when an animal is frightened of what you may be trying to do and/or is not feeling well. Working slowly and gently while reassuring your pet may lessen its fears. An animal whose behavior is uncooperative may not be the best candidate for in-hospital monitoring, but there are ways of monitoring at home that will still yield useful information for the veterinarian treating him or her. (See chapters 8 and 11.)

Pets can pick up on our feelings, and if we are nervous and unsure, they can sense this. They will often take advantage of that fact. One client of mine was afraid of being bitten by her beloved but rather aggressive cat. She still wanted to give him a chance at treatment. Before giving the insulin injection she would slip an Elizabethan collar (e-collar) on her cat, thus preventing the cat from turning around and biting her. This enabled her to give the insulin injections quickly and with confidence. In time, the collar was no longer needed, as her cat learned that nothing bad was going to happen and that a tasty meal was given at the same time. Thor lived with diabetes for eight years and passed away at the age of nineteen-years-old.

Some types of insulin may be given intramuscularly (IM). This enables the injection to be given in the rear leg of the animal, while someone is distracting the pet at the front end. This distraction may be done by speaking gently or scratching under the pet's chin or even while the pet is eating. **Not all types of insulin can be given IM, you must first check with your veterinarian** (see chapter 5).

With careful consideration given to your pet's personality and temperament, often the most difficult patient can be given a chance at treatment.

The costs involved in treating a diabetic pet

The initial costs in diagnosing and treating a diabetic pet may seem high. Costs associated with initial diagnosis and treatment can widely vary by locale. The initial cost will include exams, blood work, treatments as needed, and supplies. Usually this will decrease as your pet becomes regulated. Keep in mind that some animals are not easily or quickly regulated and the costs will be higher. Recheck exams and follow-up blood work will be needed until your pet is regulated; these tests will be done periodically thereafter. Your veterinarian may be able to give you an estimate for initial treatments but unforeseen situations and conditions may arise that will alter this. It will be helpful to come up with a realistic budget, including what you could comfortably spend on emergency treatment, if needed.

There may be frustrations as types of insulin and doses are readjusted. Insulin is not a one-size-fits-all therapy, and there may be some trial and error before finding the right type and dose for your pet. Combinations of therapies are also used. This will be more fully discussed in the next chapter.

If your pet is currently covered by pet insurance, at least some of these costs may be covered. Unfortunately diabetes is considered a preexisting condition, and you will not be able to insure a pet once the diagnosis of diabetes is made. CareCredit is another option for guardians of diabetic pets. CareCredit is a company through which you can get a medical credit card to be used for your pet. Do check to make sure that your veterinarian accepts CareCredit because some do not.

Giving Injections

One of the most common reactions to hearing the diagnosis of diabetes is the fear of giving shots to your own pet. A person's comfort level in giving insulin injections can vary widely. Although the thought of giving injections can be scary, by working closely with your veterinarian and/or veterinary technician, even the most tentative pet guardian can learn the skills necessary to do this correctly and with confidence. Since insulin syringes and needles are very small and easy to handle, many animals don't feel a thing when getting an injection. You will in time get more comfortable with doing this. Soon it will be part of a daily routine for you and your pet.

Animals requiring oral medications may be easier to treat, but giving medications by mouth is still a skill that may need to be learned by some pet guardians.

If you are not comfortable with any aspect of your pet's home treatment, do not hesitate to ask for more instruction.

Changes in Lifestyle

Many pets, especially cats, have a fairly carefree lifestyle. When we are busy, we feel it is fine spending a little less time with them. We feed and water them, take care of their basic needs, and then don't fret about leaving them on their own for a short time. Diabetic pets require more than attention to basic needs. Soon after your pet has been diagnosed, it is not advisable to leave the pet alone for a day or two. Someone has to feed, medicate, and observe your pet if you are gone twelve to twenty-four hours or more. Your pet cannot miss meals, insulin, or medications. This means changes in lifestyle that may initially put restrictions on your daily activities. You will need to spend extra time monitoring your pet's attitude, general condition, food/water consumption, and daily habits. (This will be fully discussed in chapter 8.) As success in treating diabetes involves consistency in your pet's routine, you or another trustworthy family member or caretaker will need to provide this.

In chapter 14, we will discuss when you need to leave your pet. Although caring for a diabetic pet may prove to be a challenge, determination to do the best for your pet will ensure a happy compromise for all involved.

Dealing with Emotions

Diabetes can be a frustrating disease at times. Just when you think your pet is regulated, it may experience setbacks. The disease itself is a complicated one, and every animal is different. Feeling sad, tired, scared, guilty, or frustrated is normal under the circumstances. Again, good communication with your veterinary team can help you and your pet weather any rough times you may encounter. Through knowledge and experience, they can guide and reassure you as you learn to successfully manage your pet's treatment. You may find it helpful to speak to others going through the same thing with their pets. Ask your veterinarian for a recommendation. Discuss your feelings openly with supportive friends, family members, and coworkers. Do not listen to those who belittle your feelings and emotions. Some people may even tell you that you are throwing away your money. Only those who share this special bond with animals will fully understand your feelings. In the resource section of this book, you will find many Web sites where you can communicate with others who are dealing with the same issues. It's important to note that while tips and insights gained from other pet guardians may be invaluable, you should rely on your veterinarian for medical advice.

The process of learning about and treating your diabetic pet involves an investment of emotions, time, and finances. The keys to success in treatment are consistency, good communication, patience, and decisions based on the welfare of your pet. As we travel through this book, we will learn how to do this lovingly.

Questions to Ask Yourself and Discuss with Your Veterinarian

- Are there other health issues along with diabetes, such as kidney, thyroid, and/or heart disease? Are Cushing's disease, pancreatitis, or urinary tract infections present?

- Is there a "reasonable" chance of treating and controlling the disease?

- What treatment options are available?

- If my pet (especially a cat) is indoor/outdoor, will I be able to catch them to give treatments and to monitor them?

- Am I comfortable giving injections and/or oral medications? Am I comfortable handling needles and syringes?

- Can I learn to monitor my pet at home? Would I be comfortable using a glucometer?

- If I have multiple pets, can I ensure the correct diet is being consumed by my diabetic pet?

- What are the financial considerations? Can I afford medications, insulin, syringes, additional veterinary visits, and blood work? Can I afford emergency medical care if needed?

- Do I feel the necessary treatments will improve the quality of my pet's life?

- How will this course of treatment impact my own life? Am I able to give thoughtful, consistent medical care to my pet?

- Will I be comfortable leaving my pet in the care of others if I have to travel?

CHAPTER 5

Treatment Modalities: Different Ways of Treating Diabetes

What you will learn in this chapter:

ꙮ **What initial treatments are available for diabetic pets**

ꙮ **How concurrent conditions are treated**

ꙮ **What conventional methods are used to treat diabetes**

ꙮ **What is insulin**

ꙮ **What oral medications are used for diabetic pets**

ꙮ **What integrative or complimentary therapies are used for diabetic pets**

ꙮ **What nutraceuticals are used for diabetic pets**

Initial treatments for the newly diagnosed diabetic pet

What your veterinarian will recommend for the initial treatment of diabetes depends on the health of your pet and their personal experience and/or philosophies. Some pets have diabetes uncomplicated by other health issues and are in good physical condition. Other pets are diagnosed with diabetes and are in more of a health crisis when conditions such as diabetic ketoacidosis (DKA) are present. DKA, a serious condition that affects diabetic pets, is fully explained in chapter 13. Animals suffering from DKA may be weak, dehydrated, vomiting, have difficulty breathing and have other health issues - some of which may be life threatening. Based on the information your veterinarian has gathered from a physical exam and various tests, he or she will come up with a treatment plan for your pet. By performing certain tests, your veterinarian will be able to identify and treat concurrent health issues. Although the treatment plans may vary from pet to pet, the goals of treatment remain the same—to stabilize blood glucose, make sure the pet is adequately hydrated, treat underlying conditions and causes of illness, and provide adequate nutritional support. In complicated cases of diabetes, it may not be easy to correct all health issues at once. It is often to the pet's benefit to have a slow and steady recovery.

In chapter 13, you will learn about emergency treatments for the critically ill diabetic pet.

Treatment options for the diabetic pet

There are many treatment options available for our diabetic pets these days. Pets have the benefit of not only conventional medical treatment but also of integrative or complementary medicine. (This is also called alternative medicine.) These methods include traditional Chinese medicine (TCM) and homeopathy to name a few.

Often a combination of these methods (modalities) is used. Regardless of the methods you choose, it is helpful to think of treating your animal as a whole instead of just treating the diabetes. This is the holistic way of approaching treatment. The holistic veterinary medical approach takes into account not only treating signs of disease but also supporting an animal's physical and mental well-being. Holistic veterinarians will often combine integrative methods with conventional medical treatments and formulate treatment plans specifically for each animal.

Often conventionally trained veterinarians will work along side those veterinarians specializing in integrative medicine when treating a diabetic pet. As always, good communication is a must, especially when one or more veterinarians are treating an animal.

Conventional methods of treating diabetes

Once the diagnosis of diabetes has been made, and your veterinarian decides on a treatment plan for your pet, the veterinarian will discuss with you the possible use of injectable insulin, an oral medication, and/or changes in diet.

What is insulin?

Insulin is a hormone produced by the beta cells in an organ called the **pancreas**. Insulin acts as a gatekeeper to allow glucose into the animal's cells. Without enough insulin, the animal's cells cannot absorb glucose. When glucose cannot be absorbed into the cells, it stays in the bloodstream. When there is more glucose in the bloodstream than the cells can absorb (hyperglycemia), the excess glucose spills over into the urine (glucosuria).

Insulin types vary in how rapidly they act to lower blood glucose, how long they act in lowering BG, and from which species or technology they are manufactured.

Some types of insulin are made from animal sources. Insulin of animal origin was first used in human medicine in 1922, using an extract of beef and pork pancreas. This type of insulin was approved by the FDA in 1939. Insulin made of beef origin insulin is the most similar to feline insulin. Insulin of pork origin is identical to canine insulin.

It is important to treat all animals with the insulin that closely matches their own insulin in terms of its **amino acid** structure. Insulin that is not closely matched has the potential to cause an animal's immune system to produce antibodies against the foreign insulin, resulting in possible **insulin resistance**.

Terms you may hear when learning about insulin:

Onset: This is the length of time it takes for insulin to reach the bloodstream and begin to lower blood glucose.

Peak Time: This is the time during which insulin is at its maximum strength in terms of lowering blood glucose levels.

Nadir: This is the lowest glucose level reached between insulin doses.

Duration: This is how long the insulin works to lower blood glucose

Along with its origin, insulin is also classified in terms of its actions. Most commonly intermediate and long acting insulin will be used to treat pets.

- **Rapid acting** – Onset is between five and fifteen minutes. Peak time, depending on the brand, is between thirty to ninety minutes or one to three hours. Duration is between three to five hours.

- **Short acting – Regular insulin.** Onset is one-half hour to one hour. Peak time is between two to four hours. Duration is between six to eight hours.

- **Intermediate acting – Lente.** NPH (neutral protamine Hagedorn) – Onset is between one to two hours. Peak time is between six to ten hours. Duration is ten to sixteen hours. Trade names are Humulin N (NPH), Vetsulin, and Caninsulin.

- **Long acting – Ultralente.** Insulin glargine, PZIR (Protamine zinc insulin) – Onset is between one to two hours. There is no peak. Duration is twenty-four to thirty-six hours. Trade name: Lantus (insulin glargine), and ProZinc (PZIR)

In the last few years, several insulin products have been produced and approved for use specifically with cats and dogs. Please ask your veterinarian for the latest information concerning these products. This is a market that is changing all the time!

Insulin is available in 40 u/ml (PZI insulin), 100 u/ml, and uncommonly 500 u/ml concentrations. This designates the number of units per milliliter. You will see this written as U-40, U-100 or U-500. **It is vitally important to use the correct syringe labeled for use with the concentration of insulin you are using.** Failing to do this may result in under dosing or more dangerously, overdosing, which could prove to be fatal.

Some people use conversion charts to figure how much insulin to give when using syringes that do not match the insulin they are using. Although these charts can be found on various Web sites, it is not recommended that they be used because it is easy to make a mistake resulting in possible under or overdosing.

Your veterinarian will decide on a type and dose of insulin based on his or her experience, and your pet's weight, activity level, metabolism, etc. It is very common for insulin doses to be adjusted higher or lower in the course of regulating your pet. The type of insulin also may be changed because some pets respond better to one kind or another.

Several common types of insulin used in diabetic pets:

- PZI or protamine zinc insulin has been a popular choice for treating diabetic cats because it is 90 percent beef and10 percent pork, or 100 percent beef. It was taken off the market several years ago by its manufacturer and has had several subsequent manufacturers. It may or may not be currently available. The Web site FelineDiabetes.com has a listing for sources for PZI insulin. These sources seem to change frequently so bear in mind the information on the page may include outdated information. You can find this information at http://www.felinediabetes.com/pzi-sources.htm.

- One hundred percent beef insulin is available by mail order with a veterinary prescription, although some companies will only ship directly to your veterinarian. See the resource section for more information.

- Vetsulin is made by Intervet/Schering Plough Animal Health and is an intermediate acting (lente) insulin of pork origin. In November of 2009, Invervet/Scherring Plough reported test results out of range for crystalline insulin, the longer-acting component of the two insulin components that Vetsulin contains. As a result, the company recommended that veterinarians transition pets to other kinds of insulin. As of June 2010, it is unknown when this product will be back on the market. This product alert does not pertain to Caninsulin, as it is known in markets outside of the United States.

- Insulin glargine, which is marketed by Sanofi-Aventis under the name Lantus, is a long-acting insulin and has become a popular choice of veterinarians—especially for use in cats. There have been many reports of glargine's effectiveness. Studies have shown that many newly diagnosed diabetic cats have gone into remission when this insulin is used in conjunction with a low-carbohydrate diet. Although insulin glargine is a long-acting insulin that is used once a day in humans, it is generally used twice a day in pets. Insulin glargine should not be diluted. (See chapter 10.) Cats on glargine may need to have their blood glucose monitored more closely because of the possibility of remission.

- Currently on the market is a recombinant human protamine zinc insulin (PZIR) by the name of ProZinc. ProZinc is the first long-acting protamine zinc insulin with FDA approval specifically for use in cats with diabetes mellitus. In 1982, the FDA approved recombinant human insulin, which is manufactured without using raw materials from an animal source. Insulin derived from animal sources is becoming less popular amid difficulty in obtaining raw materials and concerns over product safety. Human recombinant insulin is often a choice for treating cats and dogs, as it is often the most readily available option and is very similar to the structure of canine insulin.

Oral medications used to treat diabetes

There are several classifications of oral drugs that are given to help manage diabetes in pets.

One type of drug is in the class of **sulfonylureas**, which includes the drug Glipizide. Also called Glucotrol, Glipizide boosts production of insulin in the pancreas and may also increase insulin sensitivity by certain tissues. In order for this drug to work, an animal must have functioning beta cells in the pancreas. Figures vary widely, but this drug is thought to work on approximately 15 – 30 percent of healthy, newly diagnosed diabetic cats; however, it may take up to eight weeks to work. Although it may initially work for a cat, most cats will eventually need insulin injections. As with most drugs, there are potential side effects to be considered when using Glipizide.

Another type of drug that is used, is in the class of drugs called **biguanides,** which includes the drug Metformin (also called Glucophage.) This drug works by increasing the sensitivity of certain tissues to absorb insulin.
Current research is being done into other drugs that have the potential to help diabetic pets. Ask your veterinarian for the latest information on new drugs.

Integrative or complementary approaches to treating diabetes

One type of integrative medicine that guardians turn to in the treatment of diabetes is traditional Chinese medicine (TCM), which is a form of medicine that has been practiced in China and other parts of Asia for at least 3,000 years. It is the primary form of medicine used in China for a wide range of illnesses, while other countries view it as an alternative form of medicine. Some of the basic concepts in TCM include the balancing of yin and yang (masculine and feminine elements), as well as the balancing of energy (chi or Qi) that flows through the body. Several approaches are used to achieve good health through this balancing, including but not limited to massage, acupuncture, and herbs.

Traditional Chinese medicine views the body as a whole, instead of as separate parts to be treated individually. TCM also supports the concepts that the body needs to have a balance of energy, or it will be unhealthy and that preventative medicine helps prevent the body from getting sick.

Because diabetes is a complex disease, TCM can help alleviate health issues that insulin replacement may not address. **Acupuncture** can help by increasing blood circulation, enhancing digestion, moderating immune response, addressing pain, and mental challenges, and enabling the animal to feel better in general. It can help to facilitate exercise by reducing inflammation and stiffness. As addressed in chapter 7, animals that are able to exercise and maintain a healthy body weight have better diabetes control and often require less medication. Chinese herbs, used in formulas, can help by reducing inflammation, reducing pain, improving circulation, protecting the pancreas, providing antiglycemic properties, and regulating insulin. Traditional Chinese formulas have been developed over centuries to provide a desired effect while tempering the side effects with balancing or harmonizing and complementary herbs. This balance helps keep most formulas, when prescribed by a trained veterinarian, safe and effective for most patients.

My diabetic cat Alex benefited tremendously by TCM, including acupuncture, when treated by a compassionate and knowledgeable veterinarian who greatly improved his quality of life.

Homeopathy is another form of integrative medicine that may help the diabetic pet. Homeopathy comes from the Greek words *homeo* for similar and *pathos* for suffering and disease. Samuel Hahnemann, a German physician, founded modern homeopathy over 200 years ago.

One of the goals of homeopathy is to stimulate the body's defense mechanism to prevent or treat illness. In homeopathy, remedies are given in very small doses. According to homeopathy, these remedies would produce the same or similar signs of illness in healthy animals if they were given in large doses. The theory behind homeopathy is *like cures like*.

As with traditional Chinese medicine, treatments are individualized to each animal, taking into consideration mental, physical, and environmental factors.

Diabetic pets should be evaluated by a veterinarian/s with understanding, training, and experience with TCM, homeopathy, and other forms of integrative medicine.

Nutraceuticals that have been used in diabetic pets

Along with conventional therapy for diabetes there are several nutraceuticals that may also be helpful in treating pets with either type 1 or type 2 diabetes. These include:

- Omega-3 fatty acids – Fish oil is a source of omega 3 fatty acids and may be helpful in treating cases of diabetic neuropathy and may reduce insulin resistance. These fatty acids also reduce inflammation and can help improve joint comfort in arthritic animals.

- Gamma linoleic acid (GLA), found in evening primrose oil, has been reported to be helpful in treating diabetic neuropathy.

- L-Carnitine – This amino acid derivative can help animals lose weight while maintaining lean muscle mass. It also decreases accumulation of fat in liver cells.

- Vanadium - Vanadium is a trace mineral that can mimic the effects of insulin and/or increase how effectively the body uses it. It can reduce blood glucose levels and, in turn, reduce the amount of insulin that is given by injection. It is also thought to decrease insulin resistance.

- Chromium - Chromium is a trace mineral that is essential for insulin function. A deficiency of chromium in the body causes the tissues to not be able to utilize insulin. Chromium is also thought to reduce blood glucose levels.

- Glucosamine/Chondroitin products – While not a direct benefit in diabetes, these can be very helpful in maintaining comfort for arthritic animals, which can lead to improved exercise and quality of life. Although they do not affect blood sugar control, glucosamine products have been suggested to increase blood glucose readings, so be sure to consult with your veterinarian when using these products.

- Methyl-B12 or methylcobalamine – This vitamin has been used successfully in treating diabetic neuropathy.

In addition, there are several herbs used in the treatment and management of diabetes by holistic veterinary practitioners, often in conjunction with conventional treatments. These plant-based nutraceuticals include:

- Gymnema – This herb has been shown to promote the regeneration of beta cells in the pancreas, especially when used in combination with Zea mays (cornsilk).

- Cinnamon – Cinnamon is used in many TCM formulas and has been thought to lower blood glucose levels.

- Bilberry – Related to the blueberry, bilberry is thought to increase insulin production in pets with type 2 diabetes. It is also a powerful antioxidant.

- Panax ginseng – This herb has been shown to reduce hyperglycemia in human type 2 diabetes.

- Dandelion leaf – Dandelion leaf supports healthy liver function and can improve blood glucose control. It is an excellent source of vitamins and minerals, supplying vitamins C, B1, B2, and iron, calcium, etc.

- Burdock root – Burdock root is believed to lower blood glucose levels and exhibits antibacterial and antifungal properties.

- Fenugreek – Fenugreek is believed to lower blood glucose levels. It is an excellent digestive and kidney tonic and can be very helpful for diabetic patients that are prone to urinary tract infections.

It is very important to consult with your veterinarian before attempting treatment with even the safest and most natural products. Since the herbal and nutritional supplement market is largely unregulated, please ask your veterinarian which companies carry trustworthy and safe products.

If you and your veterinarian decide to start your pet on a new course of treatment, make sure you are comfortable with how to monitor your pet. You will need to be attentive to any changes in its behavior and/or habits that may indicate a change in blood glucose levels and/or other health issues. As always, it is best to involve everyone who is caring for your pet in monitoring for any changes.

CHAPTER 6
Keeping Your Diabetic Pet Healthy through Diet

What you will learn in this chapter:

- Why diet is an important part of maintaining your diabetic pet

- What are carbohydrates and how do they affect a diabetic pet

- What are the benefits of canned food versus dry food

- What is a raw food diet

- What type of diet should you feed your diabetic pet

- How to transition pets to a new food

- How to feed your diabetic pet

Diet

Diet it is a critical part of maintaining good health, especially for a diabetic pet. The best diet will provide not only good overall nutrition but also provide the appropriate amount of calories (supporting weight loss or weight gain if necessary), and will help to minimize fluctuations in blood glucose that occur after eating.

Pet foods should include high-quality, highly-digestible sources of protein such as chicken, turkey, beef, lamb, or fish. Protein is essential for functions like muscle growth, maintenance of tissues, reproduction, and energy. Although it is a source of much discussion, whole grains may also be added to supply complex carbohydrates that in turn supply energy. Many pet foods also include fruits and vegetables that add antioxidants, enzymes, vitamins, minerals, and fiber—all of which promote good health.

Carbohydrates 101

Carbohydrates are a component of almost every pet food and are a hot topic of conversation these days. To fully understand how carbohydrates impact your diabetic pet, it is useful to know the basics.

- Carbohydrates are compounds that include the sugars, starches, and the fiber that animals consume.

- Carbohydrates, along with proteins and fat, provide the calories in food.

- Calories are units that measure the energy level of food. All animals require a certain amount of calories everyday to function properly. The number of calories will vary depending on the general health of the animal, its environment, its metabolism, and its activity level.

- Carbohydrates, in different forms, are found in a wide range of foods, including fruits, grains, vegetables, dairy products, and legumes (beans, peas, and lentils).

- Carbohydrates (except for fiber) are transformed by the body into blood sugar (mostly glucose) and are used as a source of energy.

- Simple carbohydrates are sugars—glucose, sucrose and lactose.

  ∾ Complex carbohydrates are chains of simple sugars and are found in grains, beans, potatoes, corn, and some vegetables.

  ∾ Complex carbohydrates are generally healthier because they have vitamins, minerals, and fiber attached to them. They are digested more slowly and have less of an effect on blood glucose levels.

The term glycemic index (GI) is a term that has been used in human diabetes information since the 1980s. Although it is a term that is not used as often in veterinary medicine, it is an important concept. The GI is a numerical scale that ranks foods in terms of how high they raise blood glucose levels two or three hours after eating. The glycemic index is used for foods high in carbohydrates only and not for foods high in fat or protein because they do not cause much change in blood glucose levels. A food with a low GI will only cause a moderate rise in blood glucose, while foods with a high GI may cause blood glucose levels to rise above the recommended level.

The Glycemic Research Institute of Washington, DC, has certified several varieties in the Merrick® pet food line as being low glycemic and also named those varieties the best low-glycemic pet food of the year for the years 2005 and 2008, based on their testing of the food's glycemic index.

In 2009-2010 this same award was given to Orijen (Champion Foods) pet foods.

Do pets need carbohydrates?

There is much debate over whether cats and dogs need carbohydrates. Many veterinarians and nutritionists believe that dogs and cats can live healthfully without carbohydrates if the diet supplies enough energy in the form of glucose. Glucose can be obtained from other sources such as fat or protein. Because carbohydrates are easier to use, they are converted to energy (glucose) first before protein and fats. In this way, the amount of carbohydrates present regulates how much protein and fat will be broken down and used for energy. When there is an overabundance of carbohydrates, fat is stored instead of used. When there are not enough carbohydrates, fat will be converted and used. When there are no carbohydrates present, then fat **and** protein are used for energy.

Grain is a source of carbohydrates. Proponents for including grain in a pet's diet state that in the wild, cats and dogs eat animals such as birds and small rodents. These animals eat various seeds and grains. When a cat or dog ingests these animals, they are also ingesting the partially digested grain contents from the stomach of their prey. But this grain is vastly different from the over-processed, fractionated grains that make up the majority of some pet foods. In general, many dry foods have high levels of grain. When feeding a pet food with grains, it is recommended that it not exceed 10 percent of the total diet.

Cats and dogs are not as efficient in digesting carbohydrates as we are. They do not have enzymes in their mouth that begin to break down carbohydrates as we do. They also have a digestive tract that is much shorter than ours.

Cats and other members of the **superfamily** *Feloidea* are **obligate carnivores**. This means they have strict requirements for certain nutrients that can only be found in animal tissues, such as the amino acids taurine and arginine. Cats are designed to use protein, not carbohydrates, as their main source of energy.

Cats **must** eat meat and should never be offered a vegetarian diet. Cats especially may have trouble digesting carbohydrates. Reducing or eliminating carbs in a cat's diet usually results in improved glucose metabolism. For this reason, many cats can resolve their diabetes through diet alone.

Dogs are **taxonomically** classified as carnivores although their ability to thrive on meat, grains, and vegetables, makes them an **omnivore** in terms of diet. However, grains are neither a necessary nor an evolutionary component of their diet.

A low-carbohydrate diet will also support the health of the pancreas. The pancreas has to work overtime producing insulin to counteract the effects of too much sugar (which is produced by carbohydrates) and producing enzymes to counteract the effects of too much fat. A low carbohydrate and low fat diet places the least amount of stress on the pancreas.

Current dietary recommendations for diabetic pets point to a diet low in or absent of grain (carbohydrates) and high in protein. Many veterinary diets formulated specifically for diabetes management are based on low carbohydrates and high protein.

Fiber

Currently, there are differing opinions in veterinary medicine concerning the importance of fiber in the diet of a diabetic pet. There are benefits to adding fiber to a diabetic pet's diet. Some of the benefits include promoting weight loss, slowing absorption of glucose from the GI tract, and helping to reduce postpostprandial (after eating) rise in blood glucose. Overweight pets can benefit from fiber because it leaves them feeling more full, resulting in them eating less.

Your veterinarian may suggest adding fiber to your pet's diet or suggest feeding a diet high in fiber. Fiber can be added to the diet in the recommended form of vegetable fiber, although psyllium or grains such as cornmeal, rye, barley, oats, rice, millet, or quinoa can be added as well. These may be ground up and added to food. Canned pumpkin (not pie filling) is often recommended and many pets will not notice if it is added to their food. (Note: canned pumpkin has a high GI, you may want to chose another fiber source.) Garbanzo beans (also called chickpeas) are high in fiber and many pets enjoy their taste.

Dry foods (Kibble)

While convenient and economical for many people, diets consisting exclusively of dry foods are increasingly suspect for causing many common pet diseases such as diabetes, obesity, inflammatory bowel disease, and kidney disease. Levels of carbohydrates are often very high in dry pet food. This coupled with subpar ingredients, makes dry food no bargain when trying to offer your pet an appropriate food that will support good health throughout its life.

Cats especially should not be fed a diet of exclusively dry food. Cats are animals that originally descended from inhabitants of the desert. Their kidneys became very efficient in order to conserve water. The mainstay of their diet was fresh prey that consisted of about 70 percent moisture. The dry food that they eat now is usually in the range of 7 to10 percent moisture. Many veterinarians feel that as a result, most cats live their lives in a state of constant dehydration, which puts a strain on the kidneys and can account for kidney failure later in life.

Canned and fresh foods

Throughout its life and especially as pets age, feeding fresh and canned foods are more important as a way of getting more water into its system. These foods should at least be the majority of every older cat and dog's diet. We have created a nation of dry pet food junkies, and it is well worth persevering to find other types of foods that your pet will enjoy. Feeding fresh and canned foods will especially help diabetic pets and will help all pets avoid dehydration.

Ways of getting more moisture into your pet are:

- Canned food, all meat/no grain varieties are good choices for a diabetic pet

- Cooked chicken or turkey breast

- Low fat plain yogurt

- Cottage cheese

- Organ meats such as heart, liver, or kidneys

ᴖ Gizzards

ᴖ Steamed vegetables such as squash or broccoli. Grinding helps break down cellulose and make raw vegetables more digestible for pets.

ᴖ Green beans, pea pods, and Jerusalem artichokes are also good choices as they contain substances that are related to or may mimic insulin.

ᴖ Encouraging water consumption. (See chapter 15.)

Again, discuss any dietary changes or additions with your veterinarian.

Raw food diets

Another subject of controversy is the feeding of a raw food diet to cats and dogs. Many veterinarians and nutritionists believe that it is vitally important for animals to ingest raw meat. Raw meat foods contain enzymes and other molecules that help to digest food, provide energy, and support the repair of tissues, organs, and cells. It is my personal experience that a raw-meat-based diet fed to my diabetic cat Alex was a big part of restoring his health and enabling him to be taken off of all insulin. To supporters of this type of diet, there is no doubt that this is a more healthy and natural way to feed our pets, although there are some concerns and considerations. There are precautions that need to be taken as well as questions to ask yourself when considering if this is a diet you can safely provide to your pet.

Commercially prepared raw food diets for pets are readily available from holistic veterinarians or pet supply stores. Some people will buy raw ground meat at the supermarket and make their own food based on this. **It is extremely important to consult with a veterinarian when attempting this type of diet because nutritional deficiencies can result.** It is also a well known fact that supermarket-bought raw meat often has high levels of bacteria.

When raw food diets should not be fed:

- ❧ To animals with a compromised immune system.

- ❧ If sanitation is an issue. No one should be allowed to handle the food without **thoroughly** washing hands afterward. Food must be stored and served correctly.

- ❧ By immune compromised people. Keep in mind, that children are immune-compromised people (especially toddlers and children recently immunized).

One argument against feeding raw foods is that they are not safe for pets to eat because of certain bacteria and organisms that may be present.

Here are some basics facts to keep in mind:

- ❧ Anatomically, the digestive systems of dogs and cats are designed to handle bacteria better than ours. Their digestive systems are very short. This makes them less susceptible to harmful organisms such as E. coli, Salmonella, Campylobactor, and various parasites. This is why they can thoroughly clean their feet and other 'parts' without getting sick. (And you know where some of those parts and feet have been!)

- ❧ Humans have very long digestive systems that can hold harmful organisms for longer periods of time allowing infection to form and parasites to enter the bloodstream. This is one reason we get sick from eating things that do not affect our pets.

- ❧ Many healthy dogs and cats are not likely to get sick from Salmonella, E. coli, or Campylobacter; but they CAN pass the bacteria straight through their digestive tracts and can have it in their feces and mouths.

Benefits of a raw food diet:

◆ Healthier skin and shinier coats

◆ Can help with food allergies

◆ Can help with digestive problems

◆ Cleaner teeth and better-smelling breath

◆ Weight loss

◆ Stools will have less volume and odor

◆ Increased energy

◆ Strengthening to the immune system

◆ An excellent diet for most diabetic cats and dogs

Guidelines for serving raw food:

◞ After handling raw meat, wash your hands **thoroughly** with soap and hot water. Allow the soap to have *contact time* on your skin not a quick soap and rinse under running water.

◞ Use **hot,** soapy water to wash utensils and any surfaces used when serving this food.

◞ Discard any uneaten food after forty-five minutes.

◞ Store raw pet food so it does not come into contact with human food. (This means no drippy containers sitting in the refrigerator.)

◞ Use glass, ceramic, or stainless steel dishes and wash them thoroughly with hot, soapy water after every meal.

    ⚘ Thaw frozen food in the refrigerator and only keep it for two to three days.

    ⚘ Do not serve this or any food cold. In nature, an animal would not eat cold food. It is also not good for their digestion. Mix cold food with a little warm water or microwave it for a few seconds.

There are certainly pros and cons to the raw meat diet. But with thoughtful consideration, you can decide if this is a diet that, when served in a careful and controlled manner, will benefit your pet.

Homemade diets

More and more people are learning to make delicious and nutritionally complete homemade food for their pets. Not only can homemade diets supply a pet with all the nutrients it needs, many people enjoy the feeling of preparing this food and view it as a way of sharing their love for their pet.

A homemade diet does not simply mean feeding your pet what you eat, even if it is healthy food. Care must be taken to include all the necessary ingredients in the right proportions. Deficiencies or excesses in ingredients can result in serious heath issues.

The resource section of this book contains information on homemade diets, but your best source of information is to discuss these diets with a veterinarian who has experience with them.

What food is best for your pet?

With all the choices out there, how do you know what diet is best for your pet? Your veterinarian will most likely have suggestions for you based on what foods they have experience with. It is always a good idea to do your own research and discuss your choices with them. There are many healthy foods on the market today that will provide excellent nutrition to the entire animal while supporting specific conditions such as diabetes. When choosing a diet for your pet, consider your own philosophy on nutrition along with what will benefit your pet. If **you** would not eat by-products and unhealthy ingredients, would you want to feed them to your pet, especially considering there are more healthy alternatives? If you believe in consuming organic, fresh foods, you can choose a pet food containing only these types of ingredients. These types of food can be found at holistic veterinary offices, and pet supply stores specializing in these types of products.

In general, good choices for any pet's diet are foods free of by-products and low-quality sources of fat and protein (all of which may come from four-D animals—dead, diseased, disabled, or dying), artificial flavors and colors, as well as fillers such as corn and wheat products. Learn how to read a pet food label (see the resource section for more information), so you will have a better idea of exactly what your pet is ingesting. A good-quality source of protein should be the first ingredient; the label should say for example, chicken or chicken meal. Any grains present should be at least third or fourth on the list.

Many veterinarians feel the best diet for a diabetic pet is one that is well-balanced and provides high-quality ingredients *that the pet will reliably eat*. There is no sense in feeding your pet a food it will not enjoy and will not eat consistently, even if it is a "prescription" food. There are many choices on the market today, and if you do your homework and ask questions, you will find the right diet for your pet.

How to feed your diabetic pet

Some veterinarians will recommend **meal feeding**, which means offering a specific amount of food at a specific time. Food is put down for twenty to forty-five minutes twice daily.

Some of the benefits of meal feeding:

- Knowing the pet has eaten before giving insulin

- Food becomes a reward for getting the injection

- Decreased frequency of constipation

    ❧ Calorie control

    ❧ This is a more natural way for cats and dogs to eat

If meal feeding is not convenient because of your schedule, several types of automatic feeders for both cats and dogs are currently on the market. These can be set to dispense a measured amount of food at a specific time.

Others veterinarians may recommend **free feeding**, which means that food is accessible throughout the day and night.

Some of the benefits of free feeding:

    ❧ Animals have access to food when their blood sugar may be low.

    ❧ Avoiding aggression between pets awaiting food. (This can be solved by quickly putting food out, having several feet between bowls, and making sure each pet has its own bowl or plate.)

    ❧ Convenience for guardian or caretaker.

    ❧ Some pets like to nibble throughout the day.

You may also try a combination of feeding methods. Some veterinarians recommend meal feeding in the morning and at night, and using a timed feeder with a controlled portion of food in the middle of the day and in the middle of the night.

At least at the beginning of treatment, many veterinarians will recommend feeding your pet the way it is used to. Once your pet is stabilized, your veterinarian may recommend making gradual changes. Special attention must be paid during those times of change because blood glucose levels may fluctuate. Note, if your pet has been regulated on a diet that includes grains, you will need to monitor the blood glucose carefully when switching to a diet without them.

Some people who have dogs and cats will put the cat's food up on the counter, so the dog will not eat it. This can be a disadvantage to a hypoglycemic (low blood glucose) cat as it may feel too weak to get to the food it needs. Again, thinking creatively will allow the cat to have access to food in a way the dog does not. It may be as simple as providing the cat with a box with a small opening in which the food is placed. Then only the cat will have access to the food. See the resource section for products that are designed to help with this.

One client of mine has solved this problem by using a mesh baby gate with a small hole cut in it. The gate is used as a barrier to a small bathroom. The cat is able to go through the hole easily and enjoy its food, while the dog cannot. Note: Very motivated dogs will find a way over the gate or simply knock it over!

Transitioning your pet to a new food

Cats especially, may develop an aversion to foods offered when they are not feeling well. If you are trying to switch your pet to a new diet, do it gradually and at a time when it is in good health.

Introduce any new foods gradually and never switch an animal's food abruptly. It has been stated that cats will literally starve before they will eat a food they do not like. Never think that they should "tough it out" and will eat when they are hungry. Going without food for even a few days, can cause severe medical problems.

Basic steps for transitioning a pet to a new food:

Day 1: Mix 75 percent regular food with 25 percent new food.

Day 2: Mix 75 percent regular food with 25 percent new food.

Day 3: Mix 50 percent regular food with 50 percent new food.

Day 4: Mix 50 percent regular food with 50 percent new food.

Day 5: Mix 25 percent regular food with 75 percent new food.

Day 6: Mix 25 percent regular food with 75 percent new food.

Day 7: Serve 100 percent new food.

For some cats, this transition needs to be extended to three to twelve weeks to be successful, especially if a cat has only eaten one type or brand of food its whole life.

The best way to tell if your pet is adjusting well to its new diet is to observe its stool. Runny stool, with or without blood and/or mucus, is a sign your pet is not digesting its food well. Also be alert to any vomiting. You may have to go slower in your transitioning. If diarrhea lasts more than a day or your pet has vomited more than three times in one day, consult your veterinarian.

Nutrition is an important part of keeping your diabetic pet healthy. Remember to discuss any dietary changes you make with your veterinarian. By learning all that you can about what your pet eats, you will be helping your pet to live more healthfully. It may also have the benefit of getting you to do the same!

CHAPTER 7

Keeping Your Diabetic Pet Healthy through Exercise

What you will learn in this chapter:

ᴧ **How can exercise help a diabetic pet**

ᴧ **How to encourage your pet to exercise**

ᴧ **What are exercise dos and don'ts for the diabetic pet**

The importance of exercise

Exercise is an important part of a healthy lifestyle for all animals and can really benefit the diabetic pet. If your pet is not used to getting daily exercise, discuss with your veterinarian a plan to gradually add this to his or her routine.

Increased activity and exercise are important for several reasons:

ᴧ Exercise aids in weight loss, especially when combined with a diet that supplies the appropriate amount of calories. Your veterinarian can help you figure out the caloric recommendations that will help your pet gradually and safely take weight off. Weight loss should be a slow process taking anywhere from two to four months or longer.

- Weight gain has been shown to make diabetes worse. Exercise helps to control weight along with keeping the body's systems conditioned and in good balance.

- Exercise helps increase blood circulation. Good blood circulation is important for getting nutrients and oxygen to cells in the body. It also helps clear toxins from the cells.

- When exercising, muscles in the body use blood glucose as an energy source. As a result, blood glucose levels drop. Increased circulation due to exercise, also increases the rate of insulin absorption. **Be diligent in monitoring for signs of low blood glucose (hypoglycemia) when exercising your pet.** If out of the house, make sure that you have food with you to feed at the earliest signs of hypoglycemia. (See chapter 13). Many people take packets of honey or honey sticks with them when not at home, in case they need to get sugar into their pet quickly.

- Exercise helps muscles stay conditioned and joints stay flexible. This is especially important in the older pet. Maintaining flexibility can help reduce the chances of injury.

- Exercise helps strengthen the immune system.

- Exercise is a great form of stress relief for humans and pets alike. It can keep older pets alert and interested in the world around them.

- Exercise is great for maintaining and strengthening the bond between a pet and his or her guardian. This is your special time to be together.

- Exercise causes the release of endorphins, which are chemicals that can help reduce pain, regulate appetite, and promote happy feelings.

- Exercise promotes a better night's sleep.

Exercise dos and don'ts

- **Do** consult with your veterinarian when starting an exercise program for a pet that has not been exercising regularly.

- **Do** start slow with any exercise program. Start with five to ten minutes once or twice a day.

- **Don't** go for long walks or have extended periods of play especially when your pet is newly diagnosed or not used to that much exercise.

- **Don't** go for walks or exercise in the hottest times of the day in summer or if you live in a hot climate.

- **Do** try to exercise at roughly the same time of day and for the same length of time.

- **Do** coordinate with other members of the household to make sure the amount of exercise is consistent. You don't want to overexert your pet on some days or provide only minimal exercise on others.

- **Do** make sure anyone walking or playing with your pet knows the signs of hypoglycemia and what to do immediately when your pet exhibits them. If you take your dog to a doggy day care, make sure **everyone** there knows your pet is diabetic and knows what to do in case of hypoglycemia. (This is another reason why it is a good idea to have a tag on your pet's collar stating that your pet is diabetic).

- **Do** be sure to consult with your veterinarian about supplements or medications that can be safely used for your pet if it shows signs of discomfort during or after exercise.

Diabetic dogs and exercise

Many dogs go places with their guardians and generally have more chances for exercise than cats. It is still important to include exercise in their daily routine.

Some ways to encourage activity and exercise in dogs:

- Walking or hiking are great forms of exercise and have many benefits.

- Catching a ball, tug toy, or disc.

- Swimming. Some communities have indoor facilities for dogs to swim. Swimming is especially good for the overweight dog with joint problems.

- Play dates with other friendly dogs and/or spending time at a dog park. Your veterinarian may be able to put you in touch with other guardians of diabetic dogs. This is a great way to start your own play group and support system. (This is also a great way to meet others who understand diabetes and may be available for pet sitting.)

- Providing toys that help keep dogs more active and stimulate them mentally. There are many kinds of toys on the market that turn playtime into a fun challenge when dogs have to work at solving a puzzle or extracting a hidden treat. These types of "foraging" toys can be purchased or easily made at home. Treat balls are a good way to make pets work for their food. A treat ball dispenses food through a small opening when the pet rolls or bats at it to make the food fall out.

Diabetic cats and exercise

Although it is safer, cats that live exclusively indoors are at a greater risk for living a sedentary lifestyle that contributes to inactivity and weight gain. Cats by nature sleep a great portion of the day. This is made worse by living in an environment that provides little or no stimulation. Providing outlets for a cat's hunting and prowling behaviors can benefit your cat both mentally and physically. Daily play sessions are a great way to encourage a cat to engage its natural instincts. Providing stimulation in the form of sight and sound when cats are home alone can also add enrichment to the environment. Please see the resource section for information on the Ohio State Indoor Cat Initiative.

Ways to encourage exercise and activity in your cat:

- Play with your cat! Play sessions of 5 -10 minutes twice a day are recommended. Many cats love interactive toys to jump at and chase. These are toys that have feathers, twisted cardboard, or leather strips dangling from a wand. Many cats love to chase the beam of a laser pointer. One cat of mine loved to jump at and try to capture a furry mouse tied to the long string on a helium balloon! (Note: Supervise your cat while playing this fun game, the string could be ingested.)

- Provide a variety of toys. You can buy or make your own cat toys. Many cats love toys that rattle or crinkle. Toys stuffed with honeysuckle or catnip can be very stimulating. (Not all cats respond to these substances, though.) Ping-Pong balls, catnip stuffed mice, wadded up paper, plastic milk bottle caps, corks, and drinking straws are some examples of toys cats like to play with. It is best to monitor any toys or objects you give your cat and remove them if they get chewed into small pieces. A favorite game of my cats is exploring an inexpensive pop up laundry hamper filled with toys. Rotate favorite toys to increase kitty's interest in them.

- Provide foraging toys. (See above.)

- Give your cat is its own stuffed animal, roughly its size, and rubbed or sprayed with catnip. This makes a good "wrestling" partner for cats that live alone. Toys such as the Kong® Kickeroo are also excellent for this purpose.

- Along with your cat's primary food and water station, scatter treats and provide water in other locations in the house to get kitty to seek out other places to nibble and sip. You can divide your cats daily ration of food and place (or hide) it in several **easily accessible** places around the house.

- Provide paper bags containing toys, a few treats or fresh catnip inside. Let your cat "hunt" what is inside the bag.

- Provide appropriate surfaces for your cat to scratch on. This is one way cats exercise their muscles. There are many kinds of cat scratchers available made from sisal, cardboard, carpet, wood, etc.

- Create a tent of newspapers or tissue paper and hide a toy underneath.

- Provide cat-friendly places for bird watching or lounging in different areas of the house. Bird feeders placed outside windows can be an excellent incentive for kitty to do a little climbing up to a windowsill perch.

- Many cats love to be up high. Cat condos and cat trees scattered throughout the house will entice kitty away from using just the couch as its home base. Treats placed at the top of the condo or tree will encourage climbing.

- Training a cat to wear a harness and walk on a leash is a great safe way to allow your cat to go outside with you. (But never leave a cat unattended this way in your backyard.) Start slow with training because some cats will resist this. If this causes too much stress for your cat, it is best to go slower or discontinue the training.

- Take your cat outside for a walk in a stroller made just for pets! While this will not supply exercise or burn up calories, it will provide fresh air and a good mental break for cats that are exclusively indoors. Again, let your cat be the guide on whether it is enjoying this or not. Some timid cats may take time to warm up to the idea or may prefer the security of home.

ᕀ If at all possible, provide an enclosure for your cat in your backyard, outside of a window, or on a terrace. It is the author's personal experience that this is a great, safe way for cats to get fresh air, sunshine, and mental stimulation whenever they choose. These types of enclosures can be homemade or can be purchased. (The back pages of Cat Fancy magazine are a great source for information on different systems that are available.) Placing perches and resting spots inside the enclosure will make it more attractive to your cat. There are also different types of fencing you can use to secure an outdoor area for your cat.

While the diagnosis of diabetes may feel overwhelming and scary, it also provides an opportunity to improve the quality of your pet's life through healthy changes. It is a time to give thoughtful consideration to important issues such as exercise and environmental enrichment. Many people find it helps them make lifestyle changes as well. What could be better—you and your best friend as partners in good health!

CHAPTER 8

Monitoring Your Pet and Treatment Assessment

What you will learn in this chapter:

ᴥ **What are the goals of treating diabetes**

ᴥ **How to monitor your pet**

ᴥ **How to assess your pet's condition based on behavior, physical appearance, weight, food/ water consumption, and urination habits**

ᴥ **Why blood and urine glucose levels will vary**

ᴥ **What is transient diabetes**

ᴥ **What is a honeymoon period**

ᴥ **What types of tests are used to monitor blood glucose**

ᴥ **What is a blood glucose curve**

ᴥ **What is a fructosamine test**

ᴥ **How to monitor urine glucose**

The goals of treating diabetes

According to many veterinarians, the goals of treating diabetes mellitus in the dog and cat are to reduce or eliminate clinical signs and to prevent complications. Clinical signs such as excess drinking and urinating, weight loss, and lack of energy can all be monitored at home. Information that you can give your veterinarian regarding your pet's day-to-day condition can be very helpful in determining your pet's course of treatment and maintenance. Although it may be more difficult in a multi-pet home, there are ways you can specifically monitor your diabetic pet.

Pet guardians often become even more in tune with their pet's progress during treatment, and they become a great judge of how well their pet may be responding.

The first few weeks: Monitoring your pet

Occasionally a veterinarian will request that a pet remain in the hospital for the first day or two after beginning insulin injections, just to monitor the pet's reaction to the initial doses.

Once at home, you will need to be especially diligent in monitoring your pet. If at all possible, begin this at a time when you can have a long weekend or extended time to be with your pet. Make sure you are familiar with signs of blood sugar that is too low (hypoglycemia) and signs of blood sugar that is too high (hyperglycemia). Make sure you are comfortable with and have all your supplies organized, including easily accessible corn syrup, pancake syrup, or honey (along with a syringe to give it by mouth) in case you find your pet suffering from the signs of low blood sugar. This is especially important. (See chapter 13.)

If your pet has access to food all day, make sure you block places it can get trapped thus preventing them from getting to the food. Many cats like to curl up in the closet or drawers, so make sure you see them before you leave the house. Be a detective and go through the house to check for any other places they may get inadvertently stuck while you are away.

If your cat usually goes outside, you will want to reconsider this at least during the beginning of treatment. If you are not able to keep your cat inside, limit outdoor time and monitor the pet closely, at least until its diabetes is well regulated. You do not want the cat to wander off, perhaps with low blood sugar and not be able to get home. If your cat has a second home, or a neighbor's house they like to frequent, inform your neighbor about your cat's condition and ask them to alert you to any odd behavior. While cats are safest when kept inside, there are some cats that will not tolerate this. If your cat does go outside, make sure they have ID on their collar and a tag stating that they are diabetic.

After starting treatment, be patient when looking for changes in your pet. When initiating treatment and/or changing insulin dosage or type, the body needs time to adjust to the introduction or change in insulin. Often this takes a few days to a few weeks. One of the first things you may notice is a reduction in drinking and urinating. This is one of the best ways to monitor regulation so it is good to be aware of changes in the frequency and amount of drinking and urination. Coordinate information with all family members so you will have a better idea of exactly what is going on if you are not the only person who fills the water bowls and/or cleans the litter box or takes the dog out to urinate.

Other noticeable signs of regulation are a better hair coat, improved appetite, more energy (better attitude), resumption of grooming, and weight gain. These are good signs to look for and are very useful in monitoring progress during treatment.

Your veterinarian will recommend when you should come back for your pet's first recheck. At that visit, your veterinarian will examine your pet, check its weight, and recommend any blood work that should be done. He or she will also ask you questions regarding how you think your pet is doing. If you are still uncomfortable with giving injections, this is a good time to review the technique you are using. If you have been charting information bring that with you.

Several office visits may be needed to determine if your pet is regulated. If you have a pet who hates the carrier and/or car rides, this can be very stressful and reason blood glucose can be even higher. You may want to try doing in-home blood glucose testing yourself or have a veterinary technician do the testing. It also helps to familiarize your pet to a carrier and/or car travel. See chapter 14 for ways to do this.

Transient diabetes

Monitoring your cat closely is important as transient diabetes happens in an estimated 20-30 percent of cats. (Transient diabetes rarely occurs with dogs.) It can happen when blood glucose levels are lowered by weight loss and/or treatment with insulin. During this time the beta cell function in the pancreas becomes normal, starts to produce insulin, and the cat no longer needs insulin injections.

Honeymoon Period

Another occurrence to monitor for is a "honeymoon" period. This refers to a period when diabetic cats and dogs need a reduced amount of insulin or no insulin at all. It usually happens at the beginning of treatment for diabetes. It is a temporary remission, when there is some insulin secretion by the beta cells in the pancreas. It may last for weeks or months, but it usually results in the animal needing to be started on insulin injections again.

Monitoring blood glucose levels

Just like in people, your pet's blood glucose readings will fluctuate throughout the day and also from day to day. The target range for diabetic pets is usually between 100 to 300 mg/dl. If you are monitoring your pet's blood glucose at home, ask your veterinarian for the range he or she would like your pet to be in, as it may vary with different conditions.

There are many factors that cause fluctuations in blood glucose. Factors that raise blood glucose include stress (especially in cats), infection, and eating. Factors that lower blood glucose are insulin administration, not eating, vomiting, and exercise. Some medications can affect blood glucose, so always let your veterinarian know all the medications your pet is taking. It has been suggested that some medications prescribed to pets can raise blood glucose levels; they include Fluoxetine (Prozac), Furosemide (Lasix), Prednisone, Theophylline, and Levothyroxin (Thyrozine), and others.

Your pet may not always eat the same amount everyday. They may be more or less active some days. **It is difficult, unnecessary, and dangerous to keep a very tight control on your pet's blood glucose.** Remember, it is better for your pet's blood glucose to be a little too high than too low. You want to have "wiggle room" in case your pet happens to vomit or expends more energy than usual.

There are blood tests that determine what the blood glucose is at any given moment and some that determine what the average blood glucose was over the course of the past few weeks.

As with many aspects of diabetes, there are different schools of thought on when and how to test a pet's blood glucose. While some veterinarians rely greatly on information learned from a blood glucose curve (see below), others prefer different ways of monitoring a diabetic animal's progress. Most veterinarians will use a combination of the different types of blood tests, presence or absence of clinical signs, and feedback from you to determine how well an animal's treatment is progressing.

If you are using a glucometer at home (see chapter 9), try not to 'micromanage' your pet's blood glucose by too frequent testing. Discuss with your veterinarian how often they would like you to test.

The blood glucose curve

A blood glucose curve is a series of blood tests that determine what the blood glucose is at that given moment. In this test, a pet's blood glucose is measured every two hours, usually for twelve hours. This is most often done in the hospital; although some guardians become proficient at using a glucometer and will do their own blood glucose curve at home. Information gathered during this test includes whether insulin is effective or not, what is the duration of the insulin's effect, and what is the lowest glucose reading—the nadir. The nadir is when the insulin is most effective; therefore the blood glucose is at its lowest point. By reviewing the results of the curve, the veterinarian may discover that the insulin dosage given is too high or too low, not absorbed well, or the insulin is not effective for as long a time as needed. While this information is useful, there are some concerns that when the test is done in the hospital, it may not accurately portray what the blood glucose typically is for the pet. Factors that affect the in-hospital readings include the fact that some pets will not eat in the hospital, pets are not on their typical exercise or activity schedule, and/or pets may be stressed. If your veterinarian recommends an in-hospital blood glucose curve, and you do not think your pet will eat while away, ask if you should feed them before bringing them to the hospital.

Fructosamine blood tests

One type of blood test used in monitoring diabetes is called a fructosamine test. Fructosamine is a complex of specific carbohydrates and proteins found in the blood. This test is occasionally done in conjunction with a blood glucose curve. The results of the fructosamine test indicate the average blood glucose levels over the past one to three weeks. It can be especially helpful for animals who may not allow a blood glucose curve due to temperament and/or stress levels in the hospital. It gives a good overall picture of what the blood glucose levels have been over a greater period of time as opposed to a single blood glucose reading. This test is not affected by fluctuations in blood glucose due to stress but according to the American

Association for Clinical Chemistry, values can be influenced by large doses of vitamin C, by hyperthyroidism, circulating fat in the blood (lipemia), and/or the breakdown of red blood cells (hemolysis) that may occur during blood draws.

Another test called the glycosylated hemoglobin test may also be used. This test is similar to the HbA1c test used in human diabetes testing. This test gives results over an approximately eight- to twelve-week period in dogs and five to six week period in cats. The results of the test are also not affected by stress at the time of the blood draw.

In each of the two above-mentioned tests, the results will reveal whether regulation is in the good, fair, or poor range. Based on this, your veterinarian may suggest doing a blood glucose curve and/or making adjustments in your pet's insulin dose.

Urine glucose testing

Testing the urine for glucose is another way of monitoring your pet's response to treatment. It is thought that when blood glucose reaches approximately 250 mg/dl, the kidneys cannot process any more glucose, so it spills over into the urine. If your pet has been diagnosed with diabetes by doing blood work that supports this diagnosis, the glucose in the urine is most likely a result of diabetes. Urine glucose is less affected by stress, which makes it especially useful when monitoring cats. Keep in mind, though, that the urine that you are testing may have been in the bladder for hours. Because urine takes hours to be produced, the reading you get when testing is basically what the glucose level has been since the last urination.

Glucose concentration in urine can vary from time of day as well as from day to day, so it is best to test daily over the course of a week to catch any trends. You may even be instructed to test several times in one day or at different times of the day. Testing urine is helpful in determining the persistent presence or absence of glucose in the urine. This will help the veterinarian in deciding if further diagnostic testing is needed to determine the correct insulin dose.

Testing the urine for ketones is also important. When large amounts of ketones are formed, the level rises in the blood, and then, in the urine. Ketonuria is the term for this condition. Ketones may be found in the blood and urine of diabetic pets, and with other diseases. Normally, a cat or dog should have no ketones in its blood or urine. (For more information, see diabetic ketoacidosis in chapter 13.)

In chapter 11 you will learn about how you can do simple tests at home to monitor your pet.

When monitoring your diabetic pet's progress during treatment, it is helpful to use a combination of good information, as well as your intuition. If at any time you are concerned about your pet's condition, please call your veterinarian.

∾✹∾

CHAPTER 9
Supplies Needed for Home Treatment

What you will learn in this chapter:

ஃ **What supplies you will need to get started**

ஃ **How to organize your supplies**

ஃ **How to use charts and logs for recording important information**

ஃ **How to use a chart when performing an in-home blood glucose curve**

If your pet has been diagnosed with diabetes, you are probably learning not only a great deal about the disease itself but how to best take care of your pet. It will take a team effort on the part of you and your pet's veterinary staff to make sure your pet gets the treatment it needs. As discussed in chapter 8, monitoring your pet at home will give your veterinarian vital information on how your pet is doing both physically and mentally. While it may seem overwhelming at times, there are tools you can use to be organized and efficient.

Supplies to Have at Home

ஃ Any prescribed medication, including insulin. Make sure you have reviewed the correct dose (amount), how to store the medication and the way to administer it. Make sure it is kept in a convenient place. If there are small children in the home, keep the medication away from their reach. Designate a place in the refrigerator to keep the insulin. The butter compartment works great for this.

❧ Some people like to use a pill organizer in which they can measure daily medications. These can be found at pharmacies and discount stores among other places. Pill splitters, pill "pushers," and pill crushers are also handy devices that can help make medicating your pet easier. If you are having trouble administering the medication, ask your veterinary technician for his or her tips on doing this.

❧ The correct size syringes for the insulin you are using. This is very important! Make sure the syringes are kept in a convenient and safe place.

❧ A container for disposing of used needles, syringes and lancets. Sharps containers are specifically made for collecting and disposing of used needles and syringes. These are usually available from your veterinarian and/or pharmacy. The author's personal favorite container is an empty canister from disposable disinfecting wipes. The canisters have a small opening and flip-top lid. Any type of container (laundry detergent, mayonnaise jar, etc.) can be used if it has a snug-fitting or screw-on lid. Some municipalities require that sharps be stored in a red container. Local waste management companies can advise you on the acceptable way to store and where to dispose of used syringes if you are not using a sharps container. **Never put needles and syringes (even well wrapped) into your trashcan.**

❧ Make sure you have a supply of honey, honey sticks, corn (Karo®) or pancake syrup in case you notice signs of low blood sugar (hypoglycemia). (See chapter 13.) Have a syringe (without the needle) rubber banded to the bottle in case of an emergency. **Give one to two teaspoons (5-10 mls) of syrup, as needed, by mouth, in case of an emergency.** Syringes are also very handy to have in different sizes for giving liquids such as water after administering pills or capsules. They can also be used for obtaining urine from the litter box (cats) or collection cup (dogs) when testing urine glucose or obtaining a sample to take to the veterinarian.

- If you choose to keep a chart or notebook to record information, ensure that it and a pen are readily available. This will be helpful to record injection times, injection and/or medication amounts, food and water consumption, as well as observations, thoughts, or questions that arise.

- A glucometer, if you decide to do home blood glucose testing. (Also see chapter 11.)

- Reagent sticks for testing urine glucose, ketones, or both. These are available at your pharmacy or through mail order.

- Supplies for collecting urine from the litter box or from your dog. (See chapter 9.)

- Good, healthy food. Along with your pet's regular diet, you should always have an "arsenal" of special foods that your pet will dependably eat when it is being picky.

- Bach's Rescue Remedy° or FES Quintessential Flower Essence's 5 Flower Formula° are formulas that include the same blend of five flower essences. These liquid formulas can naturally and gently help reduce stress in your pet (and in you as well!) They can safely be used before giving injections, travel, veterinary visits, when testing blood glucose, or in the extreme cases when your pet is suffering from seizures or trauma. (They are not meant to replace appropriate medical care but can help while on the way to the veterinarian.)

- These products can be mixed in canned food, added to the water bowl, given by mouth (although some animals may dislike the taste), or rubbed onto the ears. If using before testing blood glucose in the area of the marginal ear vein, do not apply the formulas to the outer ear tip. The alcohol in the remedy may interfere with test results. Only a few drops are needed, whichever way you chose to administer it. It can also be added to a spray bottle of spring water (add about a dropper) and sprayed in the room, carrier, car, or area you will be doing injections and/or testing.

   ✍ Your veterinarian's phone number and an emergency number to use after regular business hours.

Many people find it helpful to designate a specific kitchen drawer, shelf, or a shoebox to keep diabetic supplies in one place.

Supplies for testing blood glucose

A glucometer is a small hand-held device for testing blood glucose. It is a very useful and inexpensive way of testing your pet's blood glucose at home. Keep in mind, though, that changes in your pet's insulin dose should never be made without consulting with your veterinarian, especially on the basis of one glucometer reading.

 Most people who home test, choose to use a glucometer made for human use and get very reliable results. There are many kinds of glucometers available. Also currently on the market, is a glucometer called Alpha Trak, which is manufactured by Abbott Laboratories. This glucometer is made specifically for diabetic pets. Please see chapter 11 for more information on glucometers. In the resource section you will also find information about Web sites that give recommendations on easy to use models.

Other glucometers manufactured specifically for pets include the iPet™ glucometer (Ulti-Med Inc.) and the GlucoPet (Animal Diabetes Management) glucometer. Information on both brands is included in the Resource section.

Along with the glucometer, you will need:

   ✍ Glucometer strips. Each glucometer requires its own specific kind of strips. Generic strips are available for some models.

Many types of strips use capillary action that actually draws the blood onto the strip. Make sure the strips are stored according to manufacturer's directions and have not expired as this will affect the blood glucose reading.

- Lancets or twenty-five *gauge* needles. Lancets are small plastic devices with a very sharp needle tip. They come in different gauges and come with a protective cap that is taken off before use. They can be used by themselves or with a lancet pen or holder. Needles can be obtained from your veterinarian. Either one can be used to get the required drop of blood needed for testing. As they get dull with each use, it is recommended to use a new one each time you test and dispose of them as you would a used needle.

- Petroleum jelly. When smeared on the ear tip, petroleum jelly helps the blood bead up and not disperse into the hair on the ear.

- Small clippers for clipping the hair from dogs or cats with very furry ears before doing the marginal ear vein blood test. (This is also a great thing to have in your first aid kit.)

- Small gauze squares or tissues. When placed between the pet's ear and your fingers it protects your fingers from accidentally being stuck by the lancet or needle. They are also used to put pressure on the ear after drawing a drop of blood. These squares do not have to be sterile. Another economical choice is to use absorbent paper toweling cut into approximately two-inch squares.

- Small penlight. When the penlight is used under the ear, it helps illuminate the marginal ear vein. It can also be used on top of the ear to visualize a raised area that indicates a vein.

- Booklet for recording readings. Many glucometers come with a booklet specifically for this, although most glucometers have the capability to store blood glucose readings. Computer programs are also available to monitor results.

↷ Treats! Give your pet a treat as a reward for cooperating when you are trying to get a urine or blood sample. When given at the time of the behavior, it also helps them form a positive association with your action. Read the label on the treats you are giving and make sure they contain no hidden sugar. Good choices are Real Food Toppers°. These are treat-sized pieces of freeze-dried chicken breast, beef, or salmon that can also be crumpled on food as a topper or with water, used to make gravy.

Charting your pet's progress

For many of us it is easier to keep track of information when we see it in print. It is often easier to catch patterns and trends when information is logged in an organized fashion such as a chart. It is also good information to show your veterinarian. When more than one person is taking care of your pet, charts are a good way to communicate information. If you are computer savvy, you might design your own chart, or you can use the chart provided at the end of this chapter. Another version is available to download on your computer at www. bddiabetes.com.

It is helpful to monitor information such as:

↷ How much insulin is being given and at what time

↷ What and how much an animal is eating

↷ How much water is being consumed

↷ How much is the pet urinating

↷ How active is the pet

↷ What is the weight of the pet

Information such as how much water is being consumed can be measured. How much an animal is urinating can be judged by how wet the litter box is or how often the dog requests to be taken out. That information, along with information on how active is the pet, can be recorded using a scale of one to five, with five being the highest.

It's also helpful to date information, so that you will know, for instance, when the insulin level was adjusted.

Observations of your pet's behavior can also reveal good information over the long run. You may find correlations between blood glucose levels and drinking/urinating. Or you may find correlations between amount of exercise and blood glucose levels. Before you know it, you will have gained valuable knowledge that will help you take better care of your diabetic pet.

Weighing your pet

As part of monitoring, weighing your pet no more often than weekly can spot trends in losing or gaining weight. Make sure you understand the guidelines your veterinarian has recommended regarding your pet's weight-loss goals. Too rapid weight loss can cause serious medical problems.

A small pet can be weighed while being held in your arms as you stand on a bathroom scale. You will then need to weigh yourself without the pet and subtract the difference. You can also use a baby or small-pet scale for pets under about thirty pounds.

For larger dogs, ask your veterinarian if you can take your dog into the office for periodic weigh-ins. This is also a good way to *desensitize* a dog that may be nervous going to or when at the veterinarian's office. Turn it into a fun time by using positive interaction, which may include petting, scritches, and a healthy treat given by a member of the veterinary staff.

Keeping a pet journal

Katy, a dear client of mine, describes her way of monitoring Gus, her diabetic cat. "I've found the tracking/recording *is* essential. I pick out a nice journal (usually cat-oriented or something bright and pretty) and then keep it open at the end of my kitchen counter, next to where I fix his food and test Gus. I date and track just about everything—brand and type of food and what's a hit and what isn't; the weather (if a storm is coming, there's an upswing in squirrelly behavior), various things that might be affecting his environment (like when the neighbors were doing remodeling or reroofing and Gus's glucose went way up during those noisy times!) I write down cute things he's done or what mood he's in that day. It has sort of become a mini journal for me as well. I have many of the completed "books" that make a nice journal of our lives together, as well as a useful tool for tracking the medical logistics, in a holistic context. It helps keep me focused and organized, bit by bit."

By being creative, you can come up with your own organizational systems for taking care of your diabetic pet. Talking with other guardians of diabetic pets is also a good way to learn tips that may be helpful. Whichever way you chose, consistency in monitoring will give you the best results. These results will lead to a happy and healthier pet, as well as knowing you are doing the best you can for your pet.

Date	Units of insulin given	Time of AM dose	Time of PM dose	Amount of food eaten	Urination Scale of 1-5 (low to high)	Activity level Scale of 1-5	Attitude	Comments:	Wt. once a week

CHAPTER 10
How to Give Insulin Injections

What you will learn in this chapter:

- How to store, handle, and administer insulin

- What are the parts of a syringe

- How to handle and dispose of used syringes

- How to give an insulin injection

- Where to give an insulin injection

- What to do if you miss a dose of insulin

- What to do if you are not sure if you have successfully injected your pet

- What to do if you give too much insulin

Finding out that your pet is diabetic can be stressful, especially when realizing you may have to give insulin injections, possibly for the life of your pet. For some people this may not be an issue as they are also diabetic themselves or work in health care and are used to giving injections. But for many people this is a new and difficult concept. Most people master this skill, although it may take a little time.

It may be helpful to take a few moments and think about what part giving insulin injections really worries you. Let me walk you through some common comments and emotions:

- ❧ **"I don't want to hurt my pet!"** Insulin syringes have very short and thin needles. Most pets barely realize they are being injected, especially when they are busy eating.

- ❧ **"I'm afraid my pet will grow to fear me."** I too felt this way with my cat Alex. What I found was that Alex grew to trust me even more. Giving his injections and testing his blood glucose became a way of life for both of us. When done with confidence and love, most pets realize that these treatments are not so bad. Giving yummy treats really helps!

- ❧ **"I'm afraid I'll do it wrong."** By asking questions and being clear on what you need to do, you will develop confidence. You may want try drawing up and giving saline injections until you feel confident enough to give insulin injections. You can ask your veterinary technician to mark off on a sample syringe exactly up to what line you should draw the insulin. Keep this as your reference should you be in doubt when you get home.

  Another thing to remember is that there are no major blood vessels in the area/s where you will be giving injections, so you need not worry about hitting a major vein or artery.

- ❧ **"I'm afraid of needles."** Having a veterinarian or veterinary technician show you how to handle and dispose of needles properly will go a long way in alleviating your fears. You may find that working slowly until you are comfortable is the best way. If you feel rushed to learn quickly, request more time or ask to work with someone else.

In 2007, the Health-Mor Corporation introduced Zöe, a reusable, needle-free insulin jet for cats and dogs. It is designed to be used with whatever U-40 or U-100 insulin that your veterinarian prescribes.

It comes in three sizes. See the resource section for how to obtain more information on Zöe.

  ⚘ **"I had a bad experience getting a shot once."** Generally speaking, injections we are given go into the muscle or layers of skin (transdermal) and with a larger needle. Insulin needles are very thin and go *under* the skin, causing much less discomfort at the time of the injection, as well as afterwards. Vaccinations and other injections may contain components that sting, insulin **does not** contain these components.

How to store insulin

Although it is recommended that insulin be kept refrigerated, it is not necessary. Check the insulin package insert or call the manufacturer for the specifics concerning the type of insulin you are using. It is thought that insulin kept in the refrigerator may keep its potency slightly longer. Heat, direct sunlight, and temperature extremes are harmful to insulin. If any of the above occur, it is best to replace the insulin with a new bottle.

If storing insulin in the refrigerator for any length of time, use a thermometer to make sure your refrigerator temperature is within its normal limits, and the normal limits stated for the storing of insulin.

If your pet is having issues with blood glucose being on the high (insulin may be old) or low side (insulin maybe too concentrated), just to be safe, start a new bottle of insulin at a time when you can monitor your pet closely.

There has been much discussion over how long to use an opened bottle of insulin. Some insulin manufacturers state that the insulin is good until the expiration date even if open and left at room temperature. Some recommend starting a new bottle every thirty days. Some veterinarians will recommend replacing the bottle sooner if there is a change in regulation because the insulin may be more or less potent toward the end of the vial. Ask your veterinarian or pharmacist for his or her recommendation based on their knowledge of the product.

How to mix insulin

Insulin is a *suspension*—meaning that particles are suspended within it. Mixing insulin correctly is vital to ensuring you are drawing up the correct amount for your pet. The cumulative results of not mixing the insulin well can result in insulin that is either less or more potent by the end of the bottle. This can be a cause of difficulty in regulating a pet and can also be dangerous to your pet if the concentration is too high.

There is debate about how easily the insulin can be damaged by improper mixing. When mixing insulin, roll it between your palms. This will ensure that damage is not done and that bubbles will not form inside the vial. Even very tiny bubbles will result in the wrong dose being drawn up.

Prefilled syringes can be stored in the refrigerator for up to thirty days. This may be done when leaving your pet at home with someone who is uncomfortable with drawing up the insulin or when boarding your pet. Pre-filled syringes should be rolled between the palms to mix them before administering. Special containers are sold for the storing prefilled syringes.

What are the parts of a syringe?

A syringe has four parts: the syringe barrel, the plunger, the needle, and the needle guard (cap).

The syringe barrel has gradations that indicate the amount of units on one side and the amount of 0.10 ccs on the other side. Note that 0.10 cc is the same as 1/10th of a cubic centimeter, and one cc is the same as one ml, which is an abbreviation for a milliliter. Therefore one cubic centimeter is the same as one millileter.

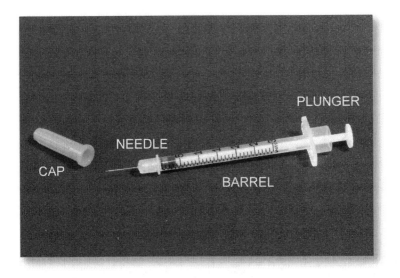

The syringes are packed individually to keep them sterile. To insure the sterility, keep the needle from touching anything before you inject your pet. Do not take the plunger all the way out of the syringe barrel and allow to it touch anything.

Syringes are designed for single use only. Some people reuse syringes, although this is not a good practice. When syringes are reused they:

- Become dull after each use and are less comfortable to your pet getting the injection.

- Increase the possibility of introducing bacteria under your pet's skin as well as into the bottle of insulin. Although insulin does contain additives to prevent this, reusing syringes is still not a good practice.

How to handle and dispose of syringes

Even the most experienced person needs to take care when handling syringes with needles. Before you give injections make sure you are comfortable handling the syringe. As a veterinary technician student, before learning to give injections, I was instructed to practice by first holding the syringe. When comfortable with that, I practiced drawing back and pushing up on the plunger, as if giving the injection. It may feel awkward at first, but with a little practice and repeating the maneuver, you can feel comfortable. It may be helpful for you to practice handling the syringe and injecting water into an orange. (If doing a practice injection on your pet, you will need to use a sterile liquid such as sterile saline solution.)

Just remember, even the most experienced veterinarians and technicians learned this very way. No one is born knowing how to give an injection!

When disposing of syringes with needles, you must also take caution to not accidentally stick yourself when replacing the cap. Insulin needles are very thin but they are still very sharp, and if attention is not paid, can go through the needle cap if it's replaced at an angle. (See chapter 9 for how to dispose of used needles.)

How to draw up the insulin

After removing the insulin from the refrigerator, you can let it set out for a few minutes to take the chill off before drawing up and injecting the insulin.

Insulin should never look thick, have clumps in it, look discolored, have floating particles, or have residue at the bottom of the vial. Some types of insulin should be clear while others are normally cloudy. Ask your veterinarian or pharmacist what is normal for the insulin you are using.

Here are the steps involved in drawing up an insulin injection.

و Mix the insulin gently, as described above.

و Remove the cap from the needle and place it close by.

و Insert the needle into the bottle of insulin and draw the plunger back to the desired dose as you have been shown. The measurement of insulin is from the needle end of the syringe to the top of the plunger, closest to the needle.

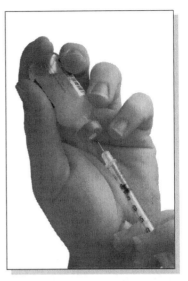

  If air bubbles are present, tap the syringe to move the air bubbles to the top of the syringe, where you can expel them by pushing slightly on the plunger. If this changes the amount of desired insulin in the syringe, draw up more insulin or start all over. It is okay to use the same syringe. Getting rid of air bubbles insures you are getting the correct dose.

Reading the gradations on an insulin syringe may be difficult as they are very thin and close together. A device called the BD Magni-Guide®, magnifies the syringe, as well as holds together the vial of insulin and the syringe. Insulin vials come in different sizes, so please check the company's Web site to see if this device will fit the type of insulin you are using.

Diluting insulin

Some people will dilute the insulin using a special sterile solution called a diluent. The advantage to diluting insulin is that it lowers the strength; therefore a larger amount needs to be given. It is often easier to draw up a larger amount, and that may also make it easier to measure the correct dose. It also gives people a better sense that the injection was given properly.

It is important to remember that by diluting the insulin, you are changing its strength and making it weaker. In other words, diluted U-100 insulin is no longer U-100 insulin. If you do chose to use diluted insulin on the recommendation of your veterinarian, make sure the vial is clearly marked. You may not be the only one administering the insulin and in an emergency situation, it is vital to know the exact strength of the insulin given.

Because multiple problems can arise by using diluted insulin, it is generally not recommended.

To feed or not to feed....

Before giving insulin injections, make sure you understand your veterinarian's recommendations for feeding your pet and the timing of injections. Your veterinarian may want you to actually see your pet eating, wait thirty minutes or so after feeding (to make sure the pet has not vomited), or in some cases, you may be confident that your pet has eaten well during the day or night.

Giving an insulin injection

Many of us were nervous the first time we gave an injection, especially when knowing that animals pick up easily on our feelings and actions. If you are feeling apprehensive about giving your first injection, remember that your pet has no idea you've never done this before! Let's pretend you are a cat or dog while the guardian handles the situation in one or two ways.

Situation A – Guardian number one is feeling nervous and fidgety. He or she desperately wants to get this over with. In the process, he or she is frustrated that the pet won't sit still. He or she keeps saying "I'll never learn to do this. I hate this, and I know it's going to hurt." The guardian fumbles for the supplies and hopes he or she is giving the right dose. Reluctantly, the guardian decides to just get it over with and gives a clumsy and tentative injection. The pet isn't sure what just happened, but it wasn't pleasant. The pet might remember this experience when in the same situation again and try to get away from it.

Situation B – Guardian number two has decided that in order to give his or her pet a healthy life, this is something he or she is going to have to master. While not crazy about the idea, the guardian has listened carefully to make sure they fully understand how to give an injection. The supplies are all at hand and the correct dose of insulin has been drawn up and rechecked. After taking a deep breath, he or she speaks softly and confidently to the pet, reassuring it that this is going to make it feel better. With more bravery than he or she really feels, the guardian quickly and confidently gives their first injection. Then he or she praises the pet for a job well done. This pet doesn't know what happened either, but it wasn't bad, and they got a treat!

Now I ask, who would *you* rather give *you an* injection? When we act confidently, our pets can sense that they are in good hands and that they will not be hurt. They will relax and most likely be more calm and cooperative. So muster all your confidence and go for it! It will only get easier.

Tips for giving insulin injections

- Use aromatherapy: Lavender is known to relax both people and animals. In spray, oil, or dried form, a few whiffs will benefit both of you! (Never use lavender on your pet—spray or sprinkle a few drops of oil or dried flowers on a towel near you and your pet.)

- If your pet is very long haired or fluffy, you can ask your veterinarian or tech to clip a "window" of fur away, so you can more easily see the skin.

- Do not sterilize the skin with alcohol. There is no need to do this, and it may cause the injection to sting, which will cause your pet to avoid getting injections. In addition, if the skin is moist with alcohol, you will not know if you have successfully injected your pet.

Restraining a pet for an injection

Although an insulin syringe has a very thin needle that most animals do not find painful, you should plan on restraining your pet until they get used to what you are doing. This also gives *you* a chance to get used to what you are doing! You may find in time though, your pet will hardly notice that they are getting an injection.

Below are 2 methods that can be used with pets that may need a little extra restraint.

In this photo Monty is being gently held so that his head is not able to turn around quickly. I am using my body as a backstop should he try to back away from what we are doing.

In this photo I have folded a towel length wise and am using it as a collar to keep Laddy in place. My hands are holding the towel in back of his head. This makes him unable to turn around to bite, from going forward or running off. This is a good alternative to 'scruffing' a cat or handling a small dog and is an excellent way to restrain for nail clipping!

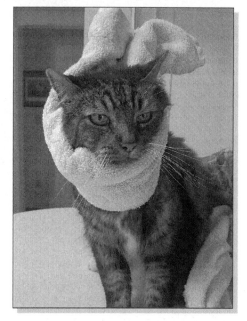

How to give an insulin injection

Have all of your supplies readily handy and your pet close by. If it is time, make sure your pet has had a chance to relieve itself and is comfortable. At least for the first few times you give an injection, it is best to have an assistant who will be calm and supportive. Wait until you pet is eating if you need to, then prepare to give the injection.

- Have the syringe filled with insulin next to you.

- After carefully removing the needle cap, hold the syringe in the hand with which you are most comfortable.

- While your assistant holds and talks reassuringly to your pet, use your free hand to pinch the pet's skin to form a tent. (Your veterinarian will advise you on the best location to give the injection.)

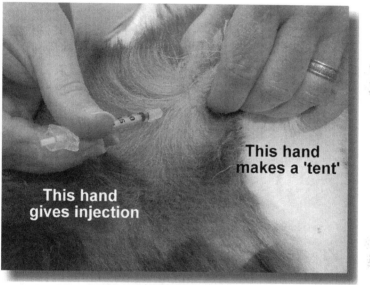

Method #1 for injecting

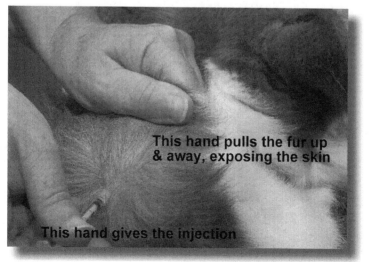

Method #2 for injecting

෯ Quickly push the needle through the skin. I like to make a clicking sound to distract the pet while doing this. Your assistant can also scratch an ear or chin to do the same thing. If it makes you tense anticipating the feel of a needle going through your skin, *briefly* look away when placing the needle under the skin to avoid transferring your fear to your pet.

෯ Gently draw back on the plunger to make sure you are not in a blood vessel. If you get blood in the syringe, remove it from your pet, discard it, and draw up a new syringe. This rarely happens, but you do not want to inject insulin into the vessel. (This is a step some veterinarians feel is unnecessary. If your pet is very squirmy and/or this is awkward for you, ask your veterinarian how he or she feels about you skipping this step all together.)

෯ If no blood is present, push the plunger in with your thumb.

෯ Remove the needle from your pet's skin and carefully place the cap on the needle. (To avoid sticking yourself, you can also discard the syringe without a cap in your sharps container. It is actually safer if you put the syringe directly into the container without recapping.)

෯ If you have successfully given the injection, you should not see or feel liquid on your pet's skin.

෯ Now reward yourself, your assistant, and your pet for a job well done!

Where to give an insulin injection

Traditionally, insulin injections have been given under the skin, subcutaneously (SC or SQ), in the scruff of the neck, roughly between the shoulder blades. (See photo.) The advantage to this location is that cats and dogs do not have very sensitive skin in this area. The skin is thick, and there is generally plenty of it.

More veterinarians are recommending that insulin injections be given in the side of the chest, the side of the belly and/or the flank area. (See photo.) The advantage to giving the injection in these areas is that the skin is thinner and the absorption of insulin may be better. An animal may be more sensitive to getting an injection in these areas and may need to be better restrained than when injecting between the shoulder blades. Restraint does not necessarily mean a headlock. You can hold an animal gently but firmly or simply scratch it on the head or under the chin. Be careful with an animal that sharply turns toward your hand as you are doing this. In this case a little more restraint may be needed.

Some types of insulin may be given intramuscularly (IM) instead of under the skin (SC). **Not all types of insulin can be given this way, so you must check with your veterinarian first.** Some types of insulin may be given both SC and IM, but the absorption will be different depending on where the injection is given. If you have been given

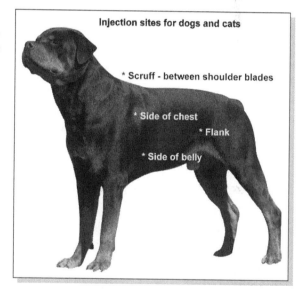

Injection sites for dogs and cats

* Scruff - between shoulder blades

* Side of chest

* Flank

* Side of belly

the approval and instructions to give insulin IM, it is very important that you stick to giving it this way. **Do not alternate giving SC and IM injections.** IM insulin injections can be given in two groups of muscles. Giving IM injections requires more instruction than giving an SC injection. You will need a demonstration by your veterinarian or veterinary technician before attempting these injections. In general, IM injections may cause a little more discomfort to your pet. An advantage to giving IM injections is that the muscle groups in which you will be injecting are toward the back of the animal and away from the face.

Ask your veterinarian specifically for their recommendation on where to give the insulin injection.

What to do if you miss or are late in giving a dose of insulin

In general, most veterinarians will say that an insulin injection can be given within an hour to an hour and a half of its scheduled time. This does not mean it is okay to give a dose an hour late and then the next dose an hour early. Try to stick to giving the injections every twelve hours, if your pet is being given insulin twice daily.

Please check with your veterinarian so you are clear on the time frame for late doses. Never try to give a partial dose a few hours later to make up for a missed dose. Skip the dose altogether and give the regular dose at its next scheduled time.

What to do if you are not sure if you have successfully injected your pet

Every once and a while you may not be sure if you have gotten the injection into your pet. Sometimes an animal may move or squirm or you may think the needle is under the skin, but it has gone under the skin and back out. (It happens to everyone, even to veterinarians and techs!) It is best to skip the injection all together and give the next dose at its scheduled time. Do not be tempted to give more insulin to make up for the missed injection. It is best to be safe than sorry and have the blood glucose be a little too high than too low. A missed dose may cause the blood glucose to be a little higher for a few days. If you are having your pet's blood glucose checked by your veterinarian close to this time, let them know about the missed dose.

You may be tempted to give a partial dose, if you realize some insulin has been deposited on your pet's skin. Again, it is best to not do this. It is impossible to know how much insulin your pet has received, so you may be overdosing them if you give more.

What to do if you give too much insulin

It is vitally important that you understand how to correctly draw up your pet's insulin dose. If you suspect that you or someone taking care of your pet has given too much insulin, you must act quickly in order to avoid a potential emergency. In another situation, you may realize that multiple insulin injections have being given. If you realize this is the case, again you must take the situation very seriously and act at once.

Here's what to do if too much insulin has been given (or you suspect too much may have be given):

- **Immediately feed your pet.** This is where your food arsenal comes in handy. If your pet won't eat, give Karo syrup or an equivalent by mouth. Give anywhere from one to three mls, depending on the weight of your pet. (Your veterinarian can give you guidelines for this based on the weight of your pet.)

- **Call your veterinarian and explain the situation.** If only a small amount of extra insulin was given, and your pet is not tightly regulated (meaning the blood glucose may already be on the high side) it might not affect your pet very much. If a larger amount was accidentally given and/or your pet is tightly regulated, this will be a more serious problem. Never the less, follow your veterinarian's instructions. You may be advised to bring your pet to the hospital for monitoring or to watch them closely at home. **It is important to remember that although your pet may seem fine at the time of the phone call, the insulin may not be at its peak of effect and the blood glucose may get much lower in a few hours.** Do not wait until you see signs of hypoglycemia, as your pet may be in serious trouble by that point.

- **After the situation is over, figure out how it happened and what you can learn from it.** Perhaps another lesson or better communication is in order. Mistakes can happen, but the important part is what we learn from them.

If at any time in your pet's treatment you have questions or concerns, consult with your veterinary team. There is a lot to learn at first, and it can seem overwhelming with all of the new skills you will need to master. It may just take time to feel comfortable and proficient. But you can do this!

CHAPTER 11

In-Home Testing Procedures for Your Diabetic Pet

What you will learn in this chapter:

- How to get a blood sample from your pet at home

- How to get good results using a glucometer

- What are urine reagent strips and how to use them

- How to get a urine sample from your pet

- What is Purina's Glucotest

- How to monitor your pet's water consumption

Doing in-home testing of blood and urine glucose gives you a chance to test your pet in the comfort of your own home, without the stress of a car trip and time at the hospital. You may decide to test on a routine basis to help monitor progress of treatment or if you think that your pet's blood glucose is too low or too high. The information you furnish your veterinarian will help him or her make the best decisions for your pet.

Testing blood glucose with a glucometer

Review the instructions regarding your specific glucometer. If you are unsure of any step, call the customer service number provided by the brand you are using. It is the author's personal experience that these calls are usually answered promptly and by a human being!

To be more successful in your testing you should:

- Choose a time when you and your pet can relax in a quiet place. The best time for testing is before insulin is given (A.M. or P.M.) or in the middle of the day—about six hours after insulin is given if you are giving insulin twice daily. Consult with your veterinarian on the timing of a midday test. You may also want to test if you think your pet may be hypoglycemic (low blood glucose.)

- Try not to hurry through the testing.

- Have an assistant help you, at least in the beginning until you feel more comfortable.

- Be familiar with your supplies and have them all laid out (including treats!)

- Take a deep breath and approach the testing with confidence. (Act like you know what you are doing and your pet will feel more confident.)

- Speak quietly and patiently to your pet.

- Remember—it only gets easier!

Keep in mind that blood glucose results taken at home, while usually accurate, may not yield the exact results as tests taken using blood drawn in the hospital. Results from blood tests vary depending on the testing method used, as well as the age and handling of the blood sample.

Getting a blood sample from your pet

Getting a blood sample from your pet is not as hard as it sounds. The amount of blood needed for a glucometer test is a drop that is roughly the size of a sesame seed. Note to nurses and veterinary technicians: even if you are proficient at drawing blood from a leg vein, resist doing this. Those veins may be needed in an emergency situation and the fewer times a needle has been inserted into them, the better. There are other places from which to get a drop of blood.

Marginal ear vein (MEV) in the cat and dog

The marginal ear **vein** runs along the outer edge of the ear and is relatively easy to see in most cases. You may be taught to use the vein itself or to prick the skin between the vein and the edge of the ear. When using the space between the vein and the edge of the ear, the blood you get will be from a **capillary**. Most human glucometers are calibrated to use capillary blood; therefore it would be more accurate to use capillary blood as opposed to blood drawn from the vein. Some human glucometers are calibrated to use blood from a variety of sites, including veins *and* capillaries. According to Abbott Laboratories, their Alpha Trak glucometer is calibrated to use either venous (from the vein) or capillary blood. It is best to check with your veterinarian and the manufacturer of the glucometer to find out exactly where they recommend drawing the blood sample. (Do not expect veterinary advice when calling a company that makes human products. Their products are recommended for use on people only.) According to Dr. Richard Nelson, Director of Small Animal Clinical Services at UC-Davis, there may be a substantial difference between using venous blood as opposed to capillary blood, so it is in your pet's best interest to perform the test as accurately as possible.

It has been reported in human diabetes information that **hematocrit**, the number of red blood cells in the blood, can affect glucometer readings. People with lower hematocrit values may have higher glucometer readings. **Anemia** is the medical condition in which red blood cell counts are lower than normal. Although supporting information is hard to find for its relevance with cats and dogs, ask your veterinarian if this may be an issue when testing your pet's blood glucose with a glucometer.

When using the MEV method, the area from which to draw your blood sample may be difficult to see at first. Especially with dogs, clipping the hair with clippers (not scissors) is helpful for hairy ears. Use caution when doing this, as the outer ear can be easily nicked, resulting in a little tear that will bleed. (Incidentally, this blood can be used to testing if you use it right away.) To stop the bleeding, apply pressure with gauze, tissue, or paper towel.

To get a drop of blood using the marginal ear vein method (MEV):

- There are several methods you can use to warm the ear, which increases blood flow. Some popular methods include placing a warm hand towel on the ear; rubbing the edge of the ear gently with your fingers; and filling a sock with rice, warming it in the microwave, and holding it next to the ear for a few seconds. Another method uses a pill bottle filled with warm water over which an ear can be neatly wrapped. Whichever method you chose, make sure the warmer you are using is not too hot before placing it on your pet's ear! You can test it on the sensitive skin on the underside of your wrist.

- To visualize the vein better, illuminate the edge of the ear with a small penlight. If you are attempting this procedure by yourself and using the penlight proves awkward, use a task light or have strong natural light behind the pet's ear.

- Apply a thin layer of petroleum jelly on the outer part of the ear to make the blood bead up and not spread through the hair. This step may not be necessary with all animals.

- Hold a small piece of paper towel, tissue, or gauze square between the pet's ear and your fingers to prevent an accidental poke by the needle.

- Have ready your lancing device or twenty-five gg needle. It may be easier if you carefully open the capped needle and lay the needle just inside the cap.

◦◦ Once the vein is visualized, gently but firmly prick the ear either on the vein or in the spot between the vein and the outer ear. A little pressure or milking motion can be used to improve the flow of blood once a drop of blood appears. The drop of blood is now ready for the glucometer strip and should be used promptly.

◦◦ Apply a little pressure with your paper towel, tissue, or gauze square to stop the flow of blood. This usually only takes a few seconds at most. Report to your veterinarian if the flow of blood seems excessive or is difficult to stop.

Alternate places that may be used to obtain a drop of blood

Other testing sites include the inside and outside of a dog's lip, or the on the underside of the paw of a cat or dog, near the largest pad. Using the paw pad is generally not recommended, especially with any animal showing sensitivity when having its paws handled or nails trimmed.

Using a nail quick is not recommended as it may likely cause pain! This in turn may cause your pet to have adverse reactions to having its paws handled and having its nails trimmed in the future.

Wherever you choose to get blood from, do not cleanse the area with alcohol, as this may interfere with the test result.

To get blood from a dog's inner or outer lip

Use caution when doing this and do not attempt if your dog is not completely comfortable with you handling its mouth. Keep in mind, dental issues and/or recent dental work may make a dog's mouth tender, so that drawing a drop of blood this way may be uncomfortable for them.

- Gently wipe the saliva off so that you have a dry surface. Using petroleum jelly is not needed in this area.

- If using the inner lip, roll the lip up toward the top of the dog's head. Using a lancet or needle, quickly prick the skin to obtain a drop of blood.

- If using the outer lip, gently roll the lip under toward the teeth and proceed as above.

- The drop of blood is now ready to use with a glucometer.

The in-home blood glucose curve

Your veterinarian may get useful information from an in-home blood glucose curve. (See chapter 8 for information on the blood glucose curve). At the end of this chapter you will find a chart you can use to gather this information. Including information such as what you pet eats and its activity level will help give your veterinarian a good idea of what your pet's day consists of and the factors that may influence blood glucose levels.

Testing urine glucose with urine reagent strips

Reagent strips are thin plastic strips that have a reagent pad on the end. The reagent pad is moistened with urine, either by dipping it into the urine, dripping urine on it using a syringe, or placing it in a stream of urine. The excess urine is gently shaken off. The resulting color on the reagent strip is compared to the chart on the container to give the test result. When using reagent strips, it is recommended to only take out one strip at a time and keep the top firmly on the container to extend the life of the strips. Do remember to occasionally check the expiration date on the container you are using. You can obtain a urine sample for testing by using any of the methods below.

Getting a urine sample from a cat

You can use the following methods if you are testing at home with strips or to obtain a sample to bring to your veterinarian. You can also place the reagent strip in the flow of urine if you are lucky enough to get there at the right time!

Method One

- Start with a clean litter box that has been washed and **thoroughly** rinsed with a lot of fresh water.

- Add nonabsorbent litter pearls, clean and rinsed aquarium gravel, plastic beads, or a product called No-Sorb® that is available from veterinarians.

- You may have to separate your cats if you have more than one, so you know exactly who used the box.

- Once you have urine in the box, pour it (and the collection material) into a **clean and rinsed** jar or container or collect it with a syringe. You can use this urine for testing with a reagent strip. If taking the sample to your veterinarian, try to get the sample there as soon as possible. You can refrigerate it if needed for a short time.

Method Two

- ⁓ Start with a clean litter box; place your cat's usual cat litter in it.

- ⁓ Slip a clear or white trash bag over the whole thing. Note: You may want to trim your cat's nails the day before you do this, so they do not shred the bag.

- ⁓ Once you have urine in the box, gently remove the plastic bag and carefully pour it into a **clean and rinsed** jar or container. You can also collect the urine with a syringe and use with a reagent strip or transfer to a container. If taking the sample to your veterinarian, try to get the sample there as soon as possible. You can refrigerate it if needed for a short time.

Method Three

- ⁓ Offer your cat a **clean,** empty litter box.

- ⁓ Once the cat has urinated, follow the directions for collection as above.

Method Four

Another excellent product to use is the Breeze® litter system by Tidy Cat. This system uses nonabsorbent pellets in a slotted litter tray. When the cat urinates in it, the urine is collected in a tray underneath that contains an absorbent pad. To obtain a urine sample, thoroughly clean the tray (it slides out completely) and replace it under the box but do not replace the absorbent pad. After the cat urinates in the box, you can pour the urine from the tray into a clean container or use a syringe to remove it.

Often cats like to void in a freshly cleaned litter box. After you have set up the litter box with the method of your choice, put your cat next to it or in it. You may be surprised with how quickly you get your sample.

Method Five

    ❧ Offer your cat a clean litter box with plain clay (not clumping) litter in it.

    ❧ Once your cat urinates in it, take a scoop of the saturated litter and add a little water to it.

    ❧ Test this liquid for glucose using a glucose dip stick.

Purina's Glucotest® Product

An alternative to taking a urine sample from home or using urine reagent strips, is the use of Purina's Glucotest® brand Feline Urinary Glucose Detection System. This system is a simple way to determine the amount of glucose in your cat's urine. Glucotest is added to the cats litter box and reacts with the urine to produce color changes in the test material. According to Purina, a higher concentration of glucose will produce a more intense color change. This helps to determine the level of glucose in the urine. The kit comes with a color chart for reading the test results. This product is available from your veterinarian or through the Internet.

Getting a urine sample from a dog

    ❧ Choose a time that your dog normally urinates or watch for their signals that it's time to go.

    ❧ Use a flat container such as pie tin or plastic food container to collect the urine. After your pet has started urinating, put the container into the stream of urine. For dogs that are low to the ground, attaching this to a handle may make it easier. You might try a broom handle, plant stake, ruler, or yardstick.

๛ If you are not successful the first time (some animals can be suspicious), wait until your pet really has to go, perhaps in another hour or so.

๛ Once the urine is collected, pour it into a **clean and rinsed** jar or container. Try to get the sample to your veterinarian as soon as possible. You can refrigerate it if needed for a short time.

You can also use this method if you need a sample for a reagent strip.

Water consumption

Increased drinking is a common symptom of diabetes. According to Drs. Edward C. Feldman and Richard W. Nelson, normal water consumption for cats and dogs varies from twenty to seventy ml/kg/day (twenty-four hours). By using the formula below, you can calculate whether the amount of water your pet is drinking is in the normal range. Remember to consider all drinking sources.

Be sure to prevent access to toilets, showers, and other unmeasured sources while you are tracking your pet's water consumption. If you have a pet that goes outside at large, it will be difficult to monitor water consumption accurately.

Water consumption will vary from pet to pet, considering the following:

๛ The health of the pet's kidneys

๛ The pet's general health

๛ The amount of canned or fresh food it consumes

๛ The climate the pet lives in

๛ The amount of exercise it receives

Conversion chart for measurements

1 kilogram (kg) = 2.2 pounds (lbs)

6 teaspoons (tsp) = 2 tablespoons (tbs) = 30 milliliters (mls) = 1 ounce (oz)

Let's use an average of 30 mls/kg/24 hours

For example – A 10-lb. cat:
       10 lbs. ÷ 2.2 = 4.5 kgs
       4.5 kgs × 30 mls = 135 mls/24 hours
       135 mls ÷ 30 mls = approx. 4.5 ounces/24hours

A cat consuming close to four to five ounces of water in twenty-four hours would be considered in the normal range.

Keep in mind that water consumption is only one variable. Your pet's good health is a combination of signs that indicate good regulation.

It is very important to discuss the results of any in-home testing with your veterinarian. Do not make any changes in the dose of insulin you are giving unless instructed to do so by your veterinarian. If at anytime the presence of ketones is detected, call your veterinarian at once.

In-Home Blood Glucose Curve for _____

Guardian: _____Date: _____

_____A.M. _____**hours after** _____**units of insulin** BG = _____mg/dl

Food consumption:

Activity:

_____**gave** _____**units of** _____ **insulin** _____**at** _____A.M.

_____A.M. _____hours after _____units of insulin **BG =** _____**mg/dl**

Food consumption:

Activity:

_____P.M. _____hours after _____units of insulin **BG =** _____**mg/dl**

Food consumption:

Activity:

_____P.M. _____hours after _____units of insulin **BG =** _____**mg/dl**

Food consumption:

Activity:

_____P.M. _____hours after _____units of insulin **BG =** _____**mg/dl**

Food consumption:

Activity:

_____P.M. _____hours after _____units of insulin **BG =** _____**mg/dl**

Food consumption:

Activity:

Weight: _____

Comments: _____

CHAPTER 12
Problems Regulating Your Diabetic Pet

What you will learn in this chapter:

∿ **What causes difficulty in regulating a diabetic pet**

∿ **How can insulin be a factor**

∿ **How can injection technique be a factor**

∿ **How can diet be a factor**

∿ **How can environment and lifestyle be a factor**

∿ **What is insulin resistance**

∿ **What medical causes may be a factor**

Despite all the best efforts, even the most experienced and conscientious pet guardian may feel frustration when his or her pet is not able to be regulated. Signs that point to a of lack of regulation are persistent or recurring clinical signs such as increased drinking and urinating, lethargy or signs of hypoglycemia and hyperglycemia, etc. There can be many reasons for this lack of regulation. Your veterinarian will recommend medical tests to rule out concurrent medical conditions that may be a cause.

It is well worth using a systematic approach to investigate any possible reasons.

Problems with the insulin itself

You can try to determine if the insulin itself is the cause of a lack of regulation by asking the following questions:

- ⚭ Is the bottle of insulin old or new?

- ⚭ Is the bottle outdated?

- ⚭ Has the insulin been properly or improperly diluted? (See chapter 10.)

- ⚭ Has the insulin gotten too warm or too cold (frozen)?

- ⚭ Has the insulin been properly stored?

- ⚭ Has the bottle of insulin been mixed properly before administering?

Your veterinarian can help answer the following questions:

- ⚭ Is there poor absorption of insulin? This may be more com- mon in cats. Poor absorption is to be suspected when a high dose of insulin does not bring blood glucose levels down. This may be resolved by your veterinarian switching your pet to a different kind of insulin. Thickening skin in places where injections are routinely given can result in reduced absorption. Rotating injection sites may resolve this. (See chapter 10 for more information on injection sites.)

- ⚭ Is the duration of effect too short? A blood glucose curve may help give this information. This too may be resolved by switching types of insulin.

- ⚭ Is the dose of insulin too low? Your veterinarian may decide to increase the dose slowly.

꒰ Is the dose of insulin too high? This may cause hypoglycemia. Hypoglycemia can cause what is termed as **Somoygi phenomenon** or rebound hyperglycemia. This is a complex chain of events that results in a dramatic increase in blood glucose. Normally, the body tries to protect itself from hypoglycemia. The body will respond when the blood glucose is too low or when the blood glucose level is within the above normal or normal range but levels fall too fast. When this happens, large amounts of stored glucose are deposited into the bloodstream, resulting in hyperglycemia. When Somoygi phenomenon is suspected, your veterinarian may decide to <u>lower</u> your pet's insulin dose.

Problems with insulin administration

There may not be a problem with the insulin itself, but with delivering it to the body. Use the following questions to help determine this.

꒰ Is a correct injection technique being used? It may be helpful for you to draw up a dose of insulin to show your veterinarian or veterinary technician your technique. Remember, they are here to help you and your pet, so don't be shy!

꒰ Is the syringe being used the appropriate size for the type of insulin you are using? For example, are U-100 syringes being used with U-100 insulin?

꒰ Are you properly using a conversion chart when using a different size syringe? (This is generally not recommended as it is easy to make mistakes. See chapter 5.)

꒰ Is an incorrect amount of insulin being drawn up in the syringe? You may want to refresh your knowledge by reviewing the picture of a syringe and how to measure the amount of insulin being drawn up. (See chapter 10.)

- Is administration of insulin inconsistent or erratic? Injections not being given on schedule and/or missed doses can affect regulation.

Problems with diet

- Is the pet being fed an appropriate amount and type of food? Could the pet be overeating or getting into another pet's food? This may be a problem with animals that go outside and forage for food at the neighbors.

- Are too many treats being given so the pet won't eat its recommended diet?

- Is the pet being fed a food containing sugars? These can often be found in treats, canned, and semi moist pet foods. Check the ingredient label of everything your pet is being fed.

Problems with Lifestyle

Environment can affect a pet in many ways. Try to be a detective and think about any possible changes to which your pet may be sensitive.

- Is your pet getting too much or too little exercise? Has exercise been inconsistent?

- Is your pet under a lot of stress or have there been changes in the household? For example, is there a new baby, new pet or house guests? Is there construction in or near your home?

- Has the pet been taken out of its normal routine? Have you been traveling or taking your pet on more outings?

Insulin resistance

Insulin resistance occurs when the normal amount of insulin secreted by the pancreas is not able to be utilized by the cells. In other words, the insulin key is not able to open the door allowing glucose to go from the blood to the cell. The pancreas continues to secrete insulin. When the cells are unable to receive this insulin, glucose builds up in the blood resulting in high blood glucose.

Insulin resistance can be caused by many factors including:

- Severe obesity. Large amounts of fat make it difficult for the muscles to absorb insulin.

- Chronic *pancreatitis*. This condition has been shown to be a possible cause of the body not fully utilizing glucose.

- *Hyperthyroidism* in cats. Hormones produced by the thyroid gland can alter glucose metabolism and increase insulin requirements.

- *Hypothyroidism* in dogs. Hypothyroidism can cause an increase in blood lipid (fat) levels, which can play a part in glucose metabolism.

- Hyperadrenocorticism, also called Cushing's disease, is a disease that is more common in dogs. In Cushing's disease, there is an excess of the hormone cortisone either by overproduction within the body or as a result of treatment with certain medications. The release of cortisone prepares an animal for a *fight or flight* situation by calling up glucose stored in the body.

- Infections of the urinary tract, skin, liver, oral cavity, etc. Infections cause the release of cortisone, glucose, and epinephrine—all of which can alter the action of insulin.

- ❧ Pregnancy and/or fluctuation of hormones in unspayed female dogs. Spaying females is important in achieving regulation.

- ❧ When some types of drugs such as steroids (prednisone, prednisolone, etc.) are given.

Although there are many variables, good communication between you and your veterinary team can help resolve problems your pet is having with regulation. Consistency, good monitoring, and patience are all necessary as you and your veterinarian determine the best course of treatment for your pet.

CHAPTER 13
Ketoacidosis and Other Unpronounceable Diabetic Emergencies

What you will learn in this chapter:

ᴧ **How to prepare for a diabetic emergency**

ᴧ **How to recognize the signs of a diabetic emergency**

ᴧ **What should I do if my pet has a seizure**

ᴧ **What are the signs of hypoglycemia and hyperglycemia**

ᴧ **How to administer glucose in an emergency situation**

ᴧ **What is Diabetic Ketoacidosis (DKA)**

ᴧ **When to call your veterinarian and what they need to know**

ᴧ **How to transport your pet in an emergency**

ᴧ **What are common emergency room procedures, including use of an IV catheter**

ᴧ **What are key points to remember in an emergency situation**

Preparing for a diabetic emergency

Guardians of diabetic pets need to be very attentive to their pet's habits and behaviors. You will need to discuss any changes and/or conditions with your veterinarian. Despite your best efforts, you may find your pet in an emergency situation, and you need to be prepared to take the appropriate steps. Familiarize yourself with your veterinarian's emergency policy. Will someone be available in the middle of the night or on holidays? If not, you will need to ask your veterinarian what options he or she recommends. They may advise you to go to your closest emergency facility or to another veterinarian who will cover in his or her place. Have the necessary phone numbers readily available for yourself and for anyone who will be taking care of your pet. It is best to have the phone numbers on your refrigerator door, by your phone, and/or in your emergency kit. If needed, call the facility ahead of time to make sure you are familiar with their hours, payment policies, and location. **Transporting your animal in a time of crisis will be much less stressful for all involved if you know exactly where you are going ahead of time.**

Diabetic emergencies can be the result of blood sugar being too low (*hypo*glycemia) or blood sugar being too high (*hyper*glycemia). Both are very serious situations that if left untreated can lead to a seizure, coma, and even death. Unfortunately, the signs of both situations can be similar.

Hypoglycemia - Low blood glucose:

Several factors will cause a decrease in blood glucose or hypoglycemia. Hypoglycemia may occur with or without signs. Hypoglycemia and its signs may occur suddenly during large increases in insulin, during a time of large overlap of insulin (in animals that receive insulin twice daily), during unusually strenuous exercise and/or following a prolonged period of not eating and/or vomiting. Hypoglycemia that occurs without signs is sometimes only found when blood work is run.

Signs of hypoglycemia include:

- confusion, disorientation, or staring into space

- fatigue, stumbling or staggering, weakness, or depression

- changes in behavior, some animals may hide

- shivering

- cats may make an odd vocalization

If you suspect your pet is hypoglycemic, give 5-10 ccs (one to two teaspoons) liquid glucose, pancake syrup, Karo® (corn syrup), or honey to your pet slowly by mouth. Be very careful when administering this because your pet may be disoriented and may accidentally bite you. Have a syringe or plastic eyedropper attached to your syrup bottle for this use.

- After giving Karo syrup, honey etc., feed your pet its normal food or something your pet will reliably eat. (This may be from your arsenal of special foods.) While the syrup will give your pet a quick sugar boost, it will not last long. Your pet will need to eat a snack or meal to keep its BG level up.

<u>Do not put liquid into the mouth of an unconscious animal.</u> Follow the instructions below for rubbing the syrup onto your pet's gums. You can also put the syrup under the tongue.

If your pet does not respond quickly, call your veterinarian and follow the instructions you are given. You may be asked to bring your pet in right away. It is very important to bring in the insulin and syringes you are using. This will be very helpful for your veterinarian in determining the amount of insulin given. If your pet has to stay in the hospital, it will be easier to have the insulin there.

Reporting any hypoglycemic episodes to your veterinarian is important, even if your pet has responded well to your treatment.

To rub syrup on an animal's gums:

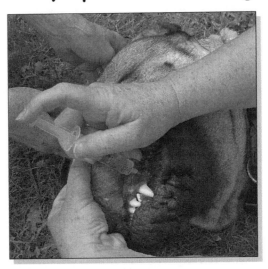

Place one hand over muzzle, lift up lip with thumb, and rub syrup onto the upper or lower gums.

Call your veterinarian immediately for further instructions.

Seizures and Diabetic Animals

Although not commonly seen, a diabetic animal may occasionally have a seizure. This is a frightening thing for even the most experienced pet owner. You may notice your pet becoming restless; vocalizing or having an odd look in their eyes. They may start running around frantically. This may be followed by an animal falling over on it's side, making rapid jaw movements, salivating, shaking it's limbs and lastly, letting lose with it's bladder and bowels. Your first instincts may be to comfort your pet by holding it. Contrary to popular belief, your pet cannot swallow its tongue. Do not have your hands or face near your pet's mouth. Unfortunately, this is a time when many people get accidentally bitten. Remove all external stimuli if possible by turning down the lights, turning off the TV or any loud music and asking any unnecessary people to leave the room. You may want to carefully place a towel or pillow under your pet's head if they are on hard flooring. Although it may seem like a long time in passing, these seizures usually last less than a minute or two. Your pet should slowly return to normal within a few minutes but they may be quiet and often very hungry after a seizure. Seizures that do not stop (Grand mal seizures) require immediate medical care. Call your veterinarian to report any seizure activity.

The Results of Too Little or No Insulin:

Too little or no insulin given will cause hyperglycemia, an increase in blood glucose. This is more of a problem in dogs. Cats can usually tolerate higher levels of blood sugar.

Hyperglycemia- High Blood Glucose:

Note: The signs of hyperglycemia can be similar to those of hypoglycemia.

Signs of hyperglycemia include:

- confusion, disorientation, or staring into space
- fatigue, stumbling or staggering, weakness, or depression
- shivering
- change in behavior
- vomiting
- increased drinking and urinating
- Reduced appetite

You may also notice that the pet's breathe smells fruity or like nail polish remover. Not everyone has the ability to smell this, although it may be present. This would indicate the presence of ketones.

Do not delay in calling your veterinarian if you notice any of these signs. The veterinarian may ask the following: What dose of insulin did you give? What time did you give it? Has your pet eaten? Has it vomited?

Note: If you are not sure if the last dose of insulin was given, do not give more.

If you are **positive** that the usual dose of insulin was not given, the veterinarian may instruct you to give it at once. Do not be tempted to give more than this dose. More is not better in this case. If your veterinarian asks you to bring in your pet for examination, go immediately. **This is an emergency!**

This may be the start of a condition called *Diabetic Ketoacidosis* (DKA)

Diabetic Ketoacidosis (DKA)

DKA is complication of diabetes. The lack of insulin results in the body being unable to take up glucose into its cells for energy. The body then feels starved, and, as a result, stored fat is broken down into fatty acids. The fatty acids undergo changes, producing ketones as a by-product. **Ketosis**, the formation of ketones, is a normally occurring process through which fats are processed for use as energy. In DKA, continual production causes high levels of ketones to be present in the urine (**ketonuria**) and/or in the blood (**ketonemia**). In response to these high levels, the body's normal respiratory and kidney functions are overwhelmed, resulting in **acidosis**. Acidosis is a condition where the acidity of the body fluids and tissues is very high. In ketoacidosis, sodium, potassium, and ketones are lost in the urine. Sodium and potassium losses result in an imbalance of **electrolytes.** Electrolytes are compounds found in the blood needed to maintain many cell functions. **Dehydration** also causes electrolyte imbalances.

Signs of DKA include increased drinking and urinating, lack of appetite, vomiting, depression, dehydration, elevated or low body temperature, panting, as well as an acetone or fruity smell to the breath. As noted above, not everyone has the ability to smell this, although it may be present.

Coexisting disorders associated with DKA are common. They include infections of the mouth, skin, or urinary tract. Inflammation of the pancreas (pancreatitis), heart, or kidney failure, and other diseases may be present.

In the beginning stages of treatment, it is very important to identify underlying causes of DKA. This will include blood work (a chemistry screen and complete blood count (CBC), a complete urinalysis, and possibly radiographs, and/or ultrasound. This will give your veterinarian a complete picture of your pet's health and guide him or her in making a therapeutic plan.

Recommended treatment for DKA starts with identifying and treating underlying causes. Primary goals are correcting dehydration and electrolyte imbalances with fluid therapy, and lowering blood glucose. Your pet may be released from the hospital when it is well hydrated, eating and drinking on its own, and has minimal or no ketones present in its urine. Your veterinarian will determine when your pet is stable enough to go home or needs to be transferred to another facility for ongoing care.

The prognosis for animals with DKA is best under the following conditions:

- There are no coexisting diseases or conditions.

- The underlying condition is easily reversed.

- The pet is presented to the veterinarian early in the disease.

- Acidosis and ketones resolve easily with administration of insulin.

Although in many cases pets may seem to recover from either a hypo- or hyperglycemic event with no apparent ill effects, it is very important to discuss the incident with your veterinarian. This information will help him or her develop a more complete picture of your pet's condition. Based on your input, your veterinarian may change the type of insulin, adjust the dose, or possibly alter the current course of treatment.

In any case, if you are not sure everything is okay or if something seems to be wrong with your pet, call your veterinarian. You will need to be partners in this treatment or it may not be successful.

You may be instructed to take your pet to an emergency facility or another hospital. If time allows, call the facility and describe the situation, the breed and size of your pet, and your estimated time of arrival. This will allow hospital staff to prepare for your arrival and notify the doctor on duty.

Transporting your Pet

In the time of a crisis, the more prepared you are, the better. An emergency situation is not the time to be rummaging through the attic to find the cat carrier or junk drawer for your dog's collar and leash. Keep these items in a place where you or anyone taking care of your pet will easily find them. Although you may want to comfort your pet on the way to the hospital, it's vital for cats and small dogs to be safely contained in a carrier or kennel. The sights, sounds, and smells of a veterinary hospital can be very frightening to animals. They may panic and try to jump out of your arms or escape from the car.

Transporting Cats:

- A cat carrier with a soft towel or blanket inside (Note: if you anticipate that your veterinarian may want a urine sample, do not put anything in the carrier. In case your pet urinates while inside the carrier, the veterinarian may be able to use urine in the carrier for some tests. An empty bladder and a wet towel can prove to be frustrating when a urine sample is needed!

∿ A ventilated laundry hamper with a **secured** top

∿ A **secured** cardboard box with holes punched out for ventilation

∿ A large pillowcase with the end securely tied. Do not use if your pet is having any trouble breathing or is vomiting.

∿ If the cat or small dog is not conscious, you can roll them (body only) in a towel and place them in a box. Use caution though. Some pets can fool you and even if they are very still, you should not assume they will stay in the box. If they get scared and adrenaline kicks in, they may be able to jump out.

Transporting Dogs:

∿ Small dogs may be transported by the same methods used in transporting cats.

∿ Medium- to large-sized dogs are best transported by collar or harness and leash. Although your dog may love everyone, in a busy waiting room at a hospital, there may be other animals that are not so well behaved. You must maintain control and restrain your dog at all times.

∿ If your dog is unconscious, secure it on a stiff surface like a covered board, shelf, ironing board, or a temporarily constructed stretcher. Secure the dog with cords or rope as it may regain consciousness in the car and start thrashing about as you are driving. If possible, have someone go with you to help safely restrain your dog.

Making a Temporary Stretcher

Create a stretcher out of a blanket, tarp, heavy-duty sheet or poncho. Lay the blanket next to the dog and slide the dog onto it. Do not roll the dog onto it. Lift the blanket, etc. from both ends.

Arrival at the Hospital and Emergency Room Procedures

When you arrive at the hospital, let the receptionist or technician know what is going on with your pet. If they are not familiar with you or if you have not called before coming, they will ask your name, pet's name, and if you have been there before.

Veterinary technicians and veterinary receptionists have been trained in *triage*, a process in which conditions are ranked in terms of priority. In medical terms, this means that the most critical cases are attended to first. Your pet will be checked immediately to see if it appears stable. The technician will assess your pet's general condition, including breathing status, color of your pet's gums, heart rate, and body temperature. If your pet appears stable, you may need to wait while a more critical case is attended to. There may be a time when the technician asks to take your pet right to the treatment area where the veterinarian will immediately examine it. This happens when the technician recognizes a sign or signs in your pet that needs immediate attention from the doctor. This can be very frightening for the pet guardian. At a time when you are worried about your pet and want to comfort it, you are asked to hand it over to someone you may not know. Be patient and let the veterinarian and support staff do their jobs. Though this may not be easy to do, this is exactly what your pet needs. In many human hospitals, parents are allowed and even expected to accompany their children. This is not often what happens in veterinary hospitals. Your waiting outside of the treatment area helps the doctor and technicians do their jobs more efficiently and with the concentration needed to help your pet through this crisis. Veterinary professionals understand your distress and will reunite you with your pet as soon as it is examined and stabilized.

What happens next depends on what the veterinarian finds when examining your pet. Your pet may be brought back up to an examination room, where you will both wait for the veterinarian to come in to speak to you. If your pet is in a life-threatening situation some treatments may be started immediately.

The first step in treating your pet is for the veterinarian to make sure that your pet's **vital signs** are stable. The veterinarian will observe your pet, listen to the rate and rhythm of the heartbeat, listen to and watch respiration, look at the color of the mucous membranes, take the body temperature, check *hydration*, and note other medical indicators of your pet's current state. As needed, measures will be taken to stabilize your pet. Once this is accomplished, the veterinarian will ask you for the history of your pet's condition. Based on this information and your pet's current condition, a course of treatment will suggested for your pet.

Your veterinarian may suggest:

- Placing an IV catheter if that has not been done already by the technician.

- Running blood tests. This will give the doctor critical information about your pet's current status. Many hospitals have the ability to do blood work within just a few minutes. This is especially important in determining current blood glucose values and identifying life-threatening situations. (See DKA.) It will also help to rule out any other illnesses that may be present.

- Starting fluid therapy if your pet is dehydrated or to correct **electrolyte** or glucose imbalances.

- Giving insulin or glucose (**dextrose**) if indicated.

- Giving medications such as drugs to stop vomiting or to control pain.

- Running an **ECG** if there are concerns about abnormal activity in the heart.

Now is the time to ask questions that will help you make the right decisions for both you and your pet. If there are terms that are used or treatments that you do not understand, ask for clarification. There are no stupid questions! If not already offered, ask for a financial estimate of the services that are being offered. Remember this is just an estimate and that costs may increase if extra treatments and/or measures must be taken to treat your pet. Be realistic about your own finances and what you are comfortable spending. Feel free in expressing these concerns to your veterinarian at this time. Be honest about these questions and concerns; it will help everyone in the long run.

Keep in mind that you and your veterinarian are a team, and good communication is very important in providing your pet with the best care possible!

What is an IV catheter and how is it placed?

An IV (**i**ntra**v**enous) catheter is a sterile flexible tube that is placed into a vein. IV catheters give immediate access to a **vein** in an emergency situation if any type of IV medication, fluid therapy, blood products (transfusion), or sedation is required. In most cases, IV catheters are not used for drawing blood samples. Usually the **cephalic** vein in the front paw is used. First the hair on the paw is clipped. The area is scrubbed with **antimicrobial** soap and alcohol is then applied. This insures that no germs will be introduced into your pet's bloodstream. While being gently restrained, the vein is *held off* by an assistant or veterinary technician. Another technician will place the IV catheter by inserting the catheter into the vein. The catheter consists of a flexible tube with a removable sharp needle that guides the catheter itself into the vein. When this is advanced into the vein and blood enters the catheter, the needle is removed, leaving the catheter in the vein. A cap is put on the end of the catheter, and it is securely taped into place. An outer bandage assures the catheter is kept clean and protected from the pet licking or chewing it. The catheter is then flushed with sterile saline solution and **heparin** (an anticoagulant) to make sure that there are no clots. Access to the vein is now readily available.

Some veterinarians prefer to place an IV catheter in the jugular vein. This allows for fluids to be administered for longer periods of time, for larger volumes of fluids to be given, and for multiple blood samples to be taken without disturbing other veins. Placement of a jugular catheter usually requires anesthesia but is usually well tolerated by most animals once in use.

Will my pet need to stay in the hospital?

Depending on the severity of your pet's situation, they will be treated and released or kept in the hospital for further treatment and/or observation. It is always hard for us to leave our pets in the hospital. Nothing feels worse than driving away without them. When intensive care and monitoring are needed, this is where your pet must be. Trained veterinarians and technicians will be attending to your pet with not only a high degree of skill but compassion and plenty of TLC. If your pet needs to stay, it may make you more comfortable to see them in their cage or kennel before you leave.

While in the hospital treatments and monitoring will be done on a scheduled basis. Monitoring includes checking your pet's general condition and making sure that your pet is warm, dry, and comfortable. In most cases it is important to get animals eating as soon as possible. Let the staff know what your pet usually eats or offer to bring in some of its favorite foods. Cats can be especially picky about eating in the hospital; sometimes bringing in their favorite food dish will encourage them to eat. It is also comforting for cats and dogs to have familiar items in their cages. You may choose to bring in an old pillow case or T-shirt that has your scent. It may not be possible to have these items returned because of the large amount of laundry done at hospitals, so please don't bring in anything you or your pet can't live without.

Before you leave, make sure you are clear on the course of treatment, approximate costs, pick-up times, and payment policies. Also make sure that you leave a phone number/s where you can be reached if the staff needs to contact you at any time.

Let the staff know if someone else will be picking up your pet to avoid any confusion.

Lastly, now is the time to take good care of you. Once your pet arrives home, it will need to be monitored, and as it has no doubt trained you to do—catered too. Easier said than done but try to relax and get some sleep. Your pet is in good hands.

Key Points to Remember in an Emergency Situation:

- **Have all of your emergency phone numbers and supplies (Leash, collar, carrier, etc.) in an easy place to find.** Teach everyone involved with your pet where to find them.

- **Stay calm.** Your pet needs for you to think and act in a way that is comforting to them. Animals can easily pick up on our feelings.

- **Keep identification on your pet.** You will also need to keep your pet safely contained or restrained all the way from your house to and into the veterinary hospital.

- **Take your pet's insulin and syringes with you when you go to the hospital.** Remember to keep the insulin cold by using an icepack wrapped in a towel or in an insulated bag.

- **Keep your pet warm if they and/or the weather are chilly.** This will be comforting to them and also help if *shock* is setting in. Use the car heater if needed. Use warm blankets and towels.

- **Know where you are going and drive safely.** You will need to pay attention to the road at a time when it is easy to be distracted. If at all possible, have someone drive you or accompany you in the car.

- **Ask questions.** The more you understand, the better decisions you will make for both you and your pet.

- **Take a deep breath.** Keep in mind that you are doing the very best for your pet at this very moment.

- **Have faith but be realistic.** The balancing act between the two can be very difficult but do your best. Your best friend depends on this!

CHAPTER 14

Getting out of Dodge: Traveling and Your Diabetic Pet

What you will learn in this chapter:

- ☙ What are special considerations of the diabetic pet

- ☙ What to consider when you are making your travel plans

- ☙ What decisions should be considered when traveling with your pet

- ☙ Why it is important to keep ID on your pet

- ☙ What is free-access crate training and how can it help your cat

- ☙ What are some suggestions for flying with your pet

- ☙ What are summer travel precautions

- ☙ How to be a good guest when traveling with your pet

- ☙ What supplies you will need for traveling

- ☙ How to find the right pet sitter or boarding facility

- ☙ What are recommendations when leaving your pet with a pet sitter, at a boarding facility, or with your veterinarian

- ☙ What anyone taking care of your pet should know and have

When I learned that Alex was diabetic, I was worried that evenings out would be a thing of the past and that I certainly would never be able to travel again. I was afraid to leave him alone. Taking care of a diabetic pet does not mean that you can't travel anymore, but it will mean new considerations. You may choose to travel with your pet or leave him or her at home with a pet sitter or at a boarding facility. Whatever you decide, there are many steps that you can take to make this as stress free as possible for you and your pet. But it is vital that you discuss your pet's health status with your veterinarian before making any plans.

If your pet is newly diagnosed, this may not be a good time to alter its habits. Changes in diet, activity level, routine, and/or any added stress will affect your pet's blood glucose levels. The severity of how this will affect him or her also depends on your pet. A dog well accustomed to car travel or who goes everywhere with its guardian will be less affected than a house cat that leaves the house only once a year to visit the veterinarian. Consider this when deciding whether or not to travel with your pet or to leave it when you are gone. Your pet may experience setbacks in regulation due to a lack of consistency in its routine.

Hitting the Road with Your Pet

If you are considering taking your pet with you, ask yourself the following questions:

- Is my pet's health stable enough for travel? You will need to involve your veterinarian in this decision.

- Will this be a positive experience for my pet?

- How much time will I get to spend with my pet?

- If you are flying, will your pet be safe and comfortable? Will it be unattended?

- Will my pet be comfortable traveling in a vehicle for longer periods of time than usual?

- Are my accommodations and places I am visiting pet friendly?

- Is my pet comfortable being in places that are unfamiliar?

- Is my pet comfortable around strangers?

- Will my pet try to run out a door or through a window if given the chance? Can I assure that they can be safely contained?

- What would I do if a medical emergency arises?

- What supplies will I need to take?

- Will I enjoy this?

Taking Your Pet with You

Begin to familiarize your pet to travel if it is not used to this. This involves gently exposing it to new people, places, and situations. Take your pet for walks and rides in the car of increasing length. Be careful not to overdo it with exercise or stress because both can affect blood glucose levels. For your safety as well as your cat's or small dog's, keep them in a pet carrier while traveling in the car. This will also feel reassuring to them as they get used to traveling this way. And always play it safe and make sure that your pet is safely restrained before opening the vehicle doors. Cats especially may try to escape quickly.

Cats can be trained to walk on a harness. Wearing a harness can also ensure safety. It is hard for a cat to wiggle out of a harness therefore harder for it to lose its collar and ID. Start slow with any new training process and use plenty of positive reinforcement and treats. Do not force your pet to do anything that it resists. You may need to go slower if your pet shows signs of stress. This may also be an indication that your pet would be happier left at home. Remember that stress is a factor in regulating a diabetic animal. Avoid this when you can!

Your pet will need an exam by your veterinarian shortly before you are to leave. Ask any last minute questions you have thought of and discuss any concerns. Discuss with the veterinarian how to avoid carsickness. In many cases withholding food is recommended, but this may not be advisable with a diabetic pet.

Taking your pet means you will need to ensure that the insulin will stay chilled en route to your destination. Insulated coolers and cold packs can be used. Wrap the cold pack in a towel so that the insulin does not accidentally freeze. See the Resources section for helpful travel products or check with your local pharmacy for specially designed containers for insulin. Taking extra supplies is also recommended. You may not be able to find the same type of insulin and/or syringes while traveling, so it's best to be prepared! If you are flying with your pet, do not pack the supplies in your luggage. Treat them as you would your own medications and carry them with you; always make sure that they are properly labeled.

The importance of identification for you pet cannot be overstated. Even if you do not anticipate being separated from your pet, you should take every precaution in case this happens. Here are some tips:

- Your pet should have a collar and tag with its name and your phone number. Make sure this is a number where you or someone reliable can be reached at all times. It may be useless if someone finds your pet and leaves a message on your home phone while you are away.

- If there is room on the tag, put your veterinarian's phone number.

- If your pet has a microchip, make sure the information you have registered is up to date.

- Make sure your pet has a tag stating it is diabetic.

There are now collars on the market that store your pet's medical information. This may be helpful for a pet that may require medical treatment in the event of being lost. Also available are metal cylinders that hold information that attach to collars. See the Resources section for more information.

Make sure your pet's traveling crate is sturdy and has no loose fittings. (Cable ties are a great way to secure any loose places.) Do not use cable ties or lock the door to the crate. You or someone else may need access in case of an emergency.

It is also a good idea to tape to the crate (with waterproof tape) information such as:

- Your pet is diabetic. Make sure this information is clearly visible.

- Your pet's basic information such as name, breed, color, and age.

- Type of insulin and dose.

- Your veterinarian's phone number.

- Your personal information and a back up contact person and phone number.

If your route is planned in advance you can check the Internet for veterinarians in the area. Call and ask about their hours and what emergency facilities are nearby. Doing this ahead of time will prevent any needless stress should your pet require emergency treatment. You may not have to use this information, but you'll have peace of mind that you are as prepared as possible. See the Resources section in this book for finding veterinarians from the Internet.

Be a Good Guest

Hotels, motels, B and Bs, and guest houses will all have different policies and fees for accommodating pets. Some require deposits or may combine the deposit with a daily fee. Some need advance notice while others gladly advertise pets are welcome with travelers. There are many excellent books written on pet friendly travel. The key is planning in advance.

Be a good guest while traveling with your pet. When staying in a hotel, motel, or B and B that allows pets, ask if your pet can stay in the room while you are not there. If so, exercise or walk your pet before you leave. If someone must come into your room while you are gone, put a sign or hang tag on the door letting anyone coming in that there is an animal present. You may want to leave the TV or radio on softly while you are gone. Make sure you make water and whatever food is in your pet's routine available. Cover the bed or furniture with sheets or towels from home. Put a towel under the water and food bowls. Keep the litter box in the bathroom and clean it often. Clean up any accidents promptly and thoroughly. Your hosts will appreciate your thoughtfulness!

Flying with Your Pet

If you are flying with your pet, it is strongly recommended that the pet fly in the cabin with you. Please check with your airline regarding regulations and costs. Keep in mind that your pet will have to be removed from its carrier or crate and go through security with you holding or leading it. In a bustling, noisy airport this can be very stressful, especially for a cat. If at all possible, ask airport security for help with this. You may request to be taken into a smaller room or area. This is another reason a harness is a good idea; it will be safer than a collar and leash should your pet try to escape.

Consider your pets comfort knowing that the carrier will have to be stowed under the seat on the plane. You may find that the carrier will be right next to a vent providing cold air or it may be overly warm.

The Humane Society of the United States (HSUS) has excellent information on the subject of flying with your pet. Included are recommendations and precautions you can take if you fly with your pet. See the Resources section of this book for the Web site for the HSUS.

Lightly sedating pets can help in this situation, although some pets can react negatively to certain medications. There are many safe, all-natural remedies you can try as well. (See Resources section.) Whatever you and your veterinarian decide is best for your pet, it is advised to try it a few days before travel so you know how your pet will react and if the dose needs to be adjusted for any reason.

Free-Access Crate Training

If you are taking your cat with you, free-access crate training (FACT) may be very helpful and comforting to your cat. Myrna Milani, BS, DVM, devised this method as an alternative way to provide a refuge for your cat. FACT is similar to crate training for dogs. The cat accepts the crate or carrier as its own safe haven. For cats, the carrier should be big enough to hold bedding, food and water bowls, and a litter box big enough for the cat. Place the carrier in a quiet and secure place in the house like your bedroom. Cats prefer to be at a height where they can look down on their surroundings. Putting the carrier on a bench or dresser may make it more attractive to the cat. (But make sure it is secure up there and not likely to fall off.) For cats that already associate the carrier with scary experiences (like trips to the veterinarian) you can start out slowly.

- ❧ First, put the carrier in a place where the cat usually rests. Take off the top and the door. Put the cat's favorite blanket in the bottom of the carrier. Create positive associations with the carrier by playing with, petting, and feeding the cat near the carrier.

- ❧ Once it accepts this, attach the top of the carrier, and let the cat get used to it too.

- ❧ Once the cat accepts both the top and the bottom, add the door. If the cat is reluctant to use the carrier, applying Feliway or lavender spray may make him or her more comfortable. You might even try a sprinkle of catnip and/or favorite treats!

FACT not only provides the cat with a refuge in your home, but it allows the cat to take its personal space everywhere it goes. Veterinary visits, boarding, travel, and moving to a new home are easier because the cat feels secure in its space. Having its own space also makes the cat less likely to feel the need to compete with other animals for territory and may help decrease fighting and urine marking. Please see the Resources section for where to find other excellent material written by Dr. Milani.

Summer Precautions!

Never leave your pet alone in a vehicle even for even a very short time. In only a few minutes temperatures can rise to over 150 degrees causing heat stroke and even death. Especially affected are short-nosed breeds such as Pekingese and Persians. Limit your travel to the cooler times of the day, before 10:00 A.M. or after 4:00 P.M. Use the air conditioner or provide plenty of cool, fresh air.

Leaving Your Pet at Home with a Pet sitter

Staying home with a pet sitter is often the best option for most pets, especially cats. Although you will not be there, your pet will have the comfort of being in its own environment with its own routine. You may even consider hiring a veterinary technician and/or experienced pet sitter to make visits to your pet and ensure its routine is followed even if some family members will still be home.

When you interview a pet sitter in your home, pay close attention to how they interact with your pet. Use your intuition when observing your pet and how it reacts to someone new. Shy pets may not warm up to someone immediately, and a patient and knowledgeable pet sitter will recognize this right away. If you are comfortable with this person, you may want to ask him or her to come at a time when you give your pet its insulin, so you can watch the sitter give it. This will also be helpful for your pet sitter to see your routine when you give the insulin. Cats especially are creatures of habit and will appreciate things being done the same way. When you interview your pet sitter, ask specific questions regarding his or her knowledge of diabetes. If you are not comfortable with the answers given, you may want to continue interviewing until you find the pet sitter that you feel most comfortable with.

If there is a worry about someone giving insulin injections correctly and your pet is regulated (and you will only be away for a few days), your veterinarian may advise skipping the insulin altogether. This may cause a temporary increase in drinking and urination that should resolve once your pet is back on insulin and regulated. But please, ask your veterinarian before discontinuing insulin injections.

It is highly recommended that you notify your veterinarian's office when you are leaving your pet with a pet sitter or a boarding facility. At this time, you should make medical and financial arrangements that will ensure that your pet receives the necessary care should you be unavailable to give authorization.

Dr. Milani offers an excellent idea for finding someone to care for your diabetic pet while you're away. "We had some guardians of diabetic cats who formed a support group for each other on their own. In addition to trading tips, they would also care for each other's cats if one was away. It worked out well for all because they all knew how to give insulin and what the other issues are. If someone is interested in forming such a group, asking the veterinarian to give their contact info to others with diabetic cats would be one way to test the waters."

How to Find the Right Pet Sitter

- Ask your veterinarian and his or her staff for suggestions. They get a lot of feedback from clients. (But bear in mind people and their pets will have an individual experience.) There may also be a technician in the hospital that does pet sitting.

- Ask your friends for the name of someone they have employed and are happy with.

- Ask a local kennel club or cat fanciers group.

- Check the yellow pages.

- Do an Internet search.

- Check references before interviewing.

When you find someone you will want to ask the following questions:

- Are you licensed, bonded, and/or insured?

- Have you treated a diabetic animal before? If so, have there been any problems?

- How will you recognize a medical emergency?

- What will you do in case of pet's emergency? What will you do in case of your own emergency?

- Will you take my pet to my veterinarian in case of emergency?

﹌ Will you be able to come at the scheduled times or will the times vary?

﹌ What questions do you have about my pet?

﹌ What are your rates?

﹌ May I call several references?

What Anyone Taking Care of your Pet Should Know and Have:

﹌ A written description of your instructions with the most important information first. Pictures are very helpful if there are multiple pets. (Also if your pet goes missing, this will be helpful in making up flyers.) Household instructions should be written on another sheet.

﹌ An emergency phone number at which you can be reached. If you are unable to be reached, is there someone else who can make decisions?

﹌ Does anyone else have a key to your home and will he or she be coming in?

﹌ What are your pet's normal habits? Do they occasionally vomit? Miss a meal?

﹌ What foods can they be tempted with if they are not eating?

﹌ Where are their favorites hiding places? Do they ever sneak outside?

﹌ Who is your regular veterinarian?

﹌ Who provides medical emergency or after hours care?

﹌ What arrangements are in place for emergency care?

- What are the financial arrangements for paying for emergency care?

- Is there a monetary limit?

- If no one is available, what are very specific instructions as to what is to be done with your pet?

- Do you want to be contacted if your pet passes away?

At the end of this chapter you will find a form you may want to photocopy and use when leaving information for your pet sitter.

Leaving Your Pet at a Boarding Facility

For people uncomfortable leaving their pet at home with a pet sitter, a boarding facility may be a good option. Discuss with your veterinarian if your pet is stable enough for this kind of environment. Boarding facilities are a good option in many cases, but you will need to decide what is best for your own pet. Many animals (usually dogs) are comfortable in new situations. They adapt well and fairly quickly. But some cats and some dogs may find this very stressful. The unfamiliar sights, sounds, and smells may be overwhelming. You may want to schedule a short stay for your pet in advance to see if it is comfortable and will eat in a new place.

There are many different types of facilities. Some facilities may even have a veterinarian or veterinary technician on the premises.

Begin looking for boarding facilities well in advance of your leaving.

Finding the Right Boarding Facility

- Call the facility you are interested in to see if the dates you wish to leave your pet are available. Call well in advance for summer vacations and holidays.

- ✍ Ask if they board diabetic pets. If so, is the staff trained to give insulin and to recognize the signs of diabetic emergencies?

- ✍ Ask who will be taking care of your pet. You want to make sure the very experienced person you meet will actually be on duty and not a less-experienced person who doesn't understand all the care your pet needs.

- ✍ Ask how long your pet will be unattended. Is there a staff member who checks on the animals at night?

- ✍ Ask what the policy is for emergency care for diabetic pets. Will they take your pet to your veterinarian or to their own veterinarian? Will they take your pet to an after-hours emergency facility?

- ✍ Visit the kennel. Visiting in person is essential. You should look at the general appearance of the facility. Is it neat and clean? How does it smell? Is the temperature comfortable? Do the animals look safely contained? What kind of bedding is provided? Can you bring your pet's own bedding?

- ✍ Feeding procedures vary with different facilities. Will you be able to ensure that they will feed the diet you provide for your pet? This is very important with a diabetic pet. Ask if there are any additional charges for special feeding arrangements.

- ✍ What kind of exercise will they be able to provide? Consistent exercise is also important to a diabetic pet, if this is what your pet is used to.

- ✍ Discuss having them give insulin. Have they done this before? Is there a special charge for this?

- ✍ Ask what their rates are. Do they offer any extra services that may be at an additional charge?

- Ask what their boarding arrangements are. What are times for drop off and pick up? Do they have a contract that states your and the facility's responsibilities?

- Ask for specific references from other diabetic pet guardians who board there, if that will make you feel more comfortable.

Boarding Your Pet with Your Veterinarian

Many veterinary hospitals offer boarding service. Start by asking your veterinarian if this is an option. A newly diagnosed pet may not be eligible for boarding but may be admitted as a hospitalized patient. Generally the difference is in the amount of monitoring, and services and fees charged. Your veterinarian can explain the levels of care involved. A boarding patient with medications is generally charged a higher fee. Hospital policies vary, so ask questions.

Questions to Ask When Boarding Your Pet at a Veterinary Hospital:

- Is my pet stable enough to be left right now?

- Will he or she need another exam before boarding?

- How will they be monitored?

- Will they be boarded or hospitalized?

- What fees are involved?

- How long will they be alone?

- Is there someone on night duty?

- If my pet is not doing well, what measures will be taken after hours?

   Will they send patients to an overnight emergency facility?

   What are hours of drop off and pick up?

   Can I bring my own medications, bedding, and food?

Leaving our pets is always hard. Perhaps this is the first time you are leaving your pet since it has been diagnosed as diabetic. Remember that pets pick up on our feelings. Make your departure as uneventful and positive as possible when leaving your pet at home or dropping them off—no matter how hard it is for you. Act as if you are only going away for an hour, although it may be longer. Leave your pet some of its favorite toys and/or something with your scent on it. Ask any last minute questions that you may have and confirm important information such as dates and times for return and/or pick up.

Now, try to relax and think about the happy reunion awaiting you when you return!

Instructions for our Petsitter

Insulin Instructions:

Insulin is kept:_____

Syringes are kept:_____

Amount of insulin given is: _____ units am _____ units pm

Where to give an injection: _____

Time(s) to give injection(s) _____ am _____ pm

Feeding instructions:

Food is kept:_____

Amount to feed is _____ am _____ pm

Treats are kept: _____

Treats may be given at:_____

Amount of treats that may be given: _____

Exercise Instructions:

Our pet is walked/let outside at: _____ for _____.

He/she really likes : _____.

He/she is not allowed to: _____.

Medical/Emergency info:

Veterinarian: _____

Address:_____ Hours:_____

Phone #: _____

Night/weekend/holiday emergency facility: _____

Address: _____   Hours:_____

Phone #: _____

<u>Directions to emergency hospital are:</u>

I can be reached at: _____ from _____ to

_____. If you cannot reach me, you may call_____

at _____.

<u>Other info:</u>

Leashes are kept at:

Pet carrier is kept:

Toys are kept:

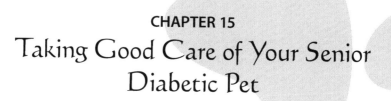

CHAPTER 15
Taking Good Care of Your Senior Diabetic Pet

What you will learn in this chapter:

- What are some physical changes your pet may be experiencing

- What can you do to make them more comfortable

- What you can do to keep them safe

- How to spot trouble and when to take your pet to the veterinarian

- How to encourage eating and drinking

There are physical changes that occur in an animal's body as it ages, in addition to any changes causes by diabetes. Around midlife (which varies widely in cats and dogs) an animal's internal systems will begin to slow down. In dogs, midlife may start anywhere from four to eight years; in cats it may start at seven years and up. Physical changes may not be very noticeable in some pets. This is why, as an animal ages, veterinary visits and periodic blood work are very important. Taking good care of your senior diabetic pet starts with understanding some of the changes your pet may be experiencing.

Some of the changes that accompany aging are:

Metabolic rate slows down. This, combined with the fact that calories consumed often exceed the energy used in the body, results in weight gain. Studies have shown that weight gain is a contributing factor to the onset of diabetes in some animals. This extra weight can also cause painful joints and can make normal ambulation more difficult. It is very Important to feed a high quality food that contains the appropriate ingredients and meets the calorie requirements for your diabetic pet. A **consistent** and **daily** exercise program (See chapter 7) can also help greatly to regulate weight and blood glucose levels as well as maintain overall good health. Occasional and excessive exercise may cause swings in blood glucose. With diabetic pets, consistency is the key to helping regulate blood glucose. Discuss these issues with your veterinarian, as diet and exercise are important factors in regulating your pet's blood glucose.

Aging pets also face a reduction the ability to regulate body temperature. As this ability diminishes, cold and wet weather can make an animal very uncomfortable. It is not recommended that pets be left outside, but if you must, special precautions should be taken by providing a dry and warm shelter. Cozy sleeping places inside will also be greatly appreciated. Many animals benefit from a heated bed as this can help with aching joints.

Circulation diminishes. Reduced circulation causes the cells in the skin to receive less oxygen. This combined with hormonal changes and less interest in grooming, can lead to dull hair coat and skin problems. Diabetic pets, whose blood glucose is not well regulated, often have a characteristic oily/flaky hair coat. As the diabetic animal becomes regulated, and its overall health improves, the hair coat often improves noticeably.

As a result of the aging process, the skin becomes less elastic and more easily damaged. Wounds that would heal quickly in a young animal may be a greater problem in an older pet. In general, the body's repair system is slower. This can also be a problem for any diabetic pet. Please notify your veterinarian of concerns about slow healing wounds or recurring skin infections. Older pets are also more susceptible to infestations of fleas, ticks, and lice. This may be due in part to a pet's lack of grooming itself. It is very important to not neglect this aspect of your pet's care. **Over-the-counter flea**

remedies are never recommended, even if they are labeled as safe to use. Many animals have been sickened or have lost their lives as a result of OTC flea products! Again, your veterinarian is the best source for advice on appropriate products for your pet.

As with all pets, frequent brushing and attention to nails is important. Report to your veterinarian any lumps and bumps that you may discover during your grooming session. You may find keeping the hair coat shorter helps your pet to stay cleaner and more comfortable. Routinely check your pet's paws to make sure nails are not growing into the pad, as this can be very painful. When animals are inactive, the length of nails may increase because they are not being worn down naturally. Often older cats will get much thicker nails and cuticles. In large dogs, overgrown nails can cause a dog to not walk properly. As a result, more frequent nail trims may be needed. (Don't forget those dew claws on dogs and extra nails on polydactyl kitties.)

Smell and taste are duller in an older pet, which can result in a poor appetite. In the older pet, there are fewer taste buds and the sense of smell may decline. This may cause a lack of appetite. There may be times when you need to tempt your pet with warmed foods and find healthy treats to stimulate appetite. Read the list of ingredients in any soft treat you want to give because many include corn syrup. Your diabetic pet does not need added sugar in its food. Use caution with the amount of treats you feed your diabetic pet. Eating regular meals is vital to maintaining blood glucose levels. Eating schedules (and therefore insulin injections) can be thrown off by consuming too many treats in between meals.

Often older pets benefit from food and water bowls that are elevated. If they have arthritis or stiffness in their neck, eating from an elevated bowl will be more comfortable for them. It may also help the older pet that is having problems with their esophagus.

Dental problems, which are often present, can make eating difficult for older pets. Tartar may build up on the teeth and push the gums back, allowing bacteria to more easily infect the gums. Large amounts of dental bacteria floating around in the bloodstream can have serious consequences on the health of the heart and kidneys. This can be especially serious for a diabetic pet. Talk to your veterinarian about what kind of dental work your pet may need. It may be a simple dental cleaning or may involve tooth extraction. Your diabetic pet will need special care from your veterinarian before this procedure. To ensure safety during anesthesia, most animals should fast before surgery. Ask your veterinarian what you need to do in terms of withholding food and adjusting your pet's normal insulin dosage. There may be addition costs for dental work for diabetics, since your pet will need to have fluids given and blood glucose monitored while under anesthesia.

Many dental problems can be evaluated at the time of your pet's physical exam. There are also signs you can watch for at home that alert you to any problems. Animals with a painful mouth may exhibit some or all of the following behaviors:

- reluctance to eat although they show initial interest in food

- chewing on only one side of their mouth

- food falling from their mouth while eating

- pawing at the side of their mouth

- taking only one or two bites of food, then walking away

- weight loss

- facial swelling

- foul smelling breath

Any of the above signs are reason to take your pet in for an exam with your veterinarian.

Eyesight becomes less acute as thickening of the lenses and occasionally cataracts may appear. Diminishing eyesight can be very serious for animals left on their own outside. For the indoor cat, this may be a reason the kitty is not making it to the litter box in the middle of the night. It is a good idea to provide lighting in places pets frequent at night, as well as safeguard animals with impaired eyesight from steps, balconies, and other places from which they could fall.

Cataracts are common in diabetic dogs but not in cats. Cataract formation may happen quickly in dogs, in a matter of days, or it may take years. Once formed, cataracts are irreversible but can be surgically removed by a veterinary ophthalmologist. There is generally a high success rate in restoring vision with this procedure, although there are several factors that determine success. These factors include how well regulated the dog's blood sugar is, and the general health of the eye. A veterinary ophthalmologist can discuss your dog's medical status with you to determine if your pet would be a good surgical candidate.

Other eye problems noted in the diabetic pet include ulcerations and inflammations, and slow-healing wounds and lesions. This is another reason why periodic exams are very important.

Hearing becomes less acute and internal changes may make the hearing less sensitive. Wax may also build up dulling sounds that get through. Your veterinarian can examine your pet's ears with an **otoscope** to make sure there is not a medical problem (infection, ear mites, wax, or growths) that may be the reason for hearing loss.

Be careful to not startle a sleeping pet that may not hear you. Be very careful with outdoor pets when starting up and moving cars. Also be aware that your pet may not hear you calling, and you will need extra patience and perhaps another system besides your voice for keeping them close to you on walks or when out in the backyard.

The digestive system may encounter changes and feeding smaller meals may be easier on your pet's system. Keep in mind there are different philosophies on how best to feed your diabetic pet. (See chapter 6) With your veterinarian's help, you can determine which method is best for feeding your pet. Again, consistency is very important and you may be advised to feed your pet as it is accustomed.

Constipation may also be a problem in the older pet. Talk to your veterinarian if you think your pet appears to be constipated, even occasionally, as the problem is much easier to treat if noticed early and prevented before it becomes severe. If several people are walking the dog or cleaning the litter box, devise a system so that you know exactly what your pet's fecal output is.

Tangled hair under the tail can be a reason for constipation. If the pet is not able to defecate normally, the stool may back up. The longer stool stays in body, the harder and more difficult to pass it becomes. It is recommended to use clippers, as opposed to scissors, to remove long hair in this area. If you do not have clippers, a groomer or vet tech can clip the hair for you.

You may have to occasionally separate animals so you get a better idea of who is doing what in regard to bowel movements. Some cats will void in a freshly cleaned litter box, so placing them in it right after cleaning, can sometimes give you your answer quickly!

Adding fiber to the diet is often recommended for this. Psyllium and even garbanzo beans (also called chickpeas), added to your pet's canned food, are a way of getting more fiber into your pet. Canned pumpkin, which is often recommended for constipation, may not be the best choice for a diabetic pet because of its high *glycemic indices.* Again, run any dietary additions and/or changes by your veterinarian first, as diet is an important aspect of caring for your diabetic pet. Your veterinarian can also prescribe laxatives that are gentle and easy to use. Never use enemas or laxatives from the drugstore without discussing this with your veterinarian first. Encouraging water consumption is also important to avoid constipation. (See below.)

Feeding a high quality food with healthy ingredients (no artificial flavors, colors, or by-products) will not only support your pet's overall good health but may be easier for sensitive digestive systems.

Muscle tone and volume diminishes, making the animal move more slowly and with less agility. Both dogs and cats can suffer from arthritis. Provide ramps, stairs, or step stools so those pets will have an easier time getting on the couch, bed, or in the car. Use rubber-backed rugs or mats throughout the house to give your pet a nonslip surface on smooth flooring. There are a number of nutritional supplements and medications to help arthritic animals with their pain. **Never use human pain medication without discussing it with your veterinarian first.** Cats in particular can be poisoned by some human pain medications.

For elderly cats, cutting down the sides of the litter box will make it easier for the cat to step into it. An under the bed sweater box makes a great low-sided and large litter box, perfect for elderly cats. Keep the cat litter to only about one and one half inches to make it easier for kitty to get its footing inside the box.

Some diabetic pets, most commonly cats, will develop what is called a diabetic *neuropathy*. This may be mistaken for muscle weakness. The animal has what is described as a *plantigrade* stance. Think of how a bear walks down on its feet as opposed to on its toes, or it may be weak or wobbly in the hind limbs. This is a complicated physiological process that is very closely related to how well the blood glucose is regulated and may be a transient condition. There is a form of vitamin B that has proved beneficial to animals with this condition. (Please see chapter 5).

The urinary system may experience some changes. Diabetic pets may be more prone to urinary infections because of the increase in sugar in the urine. It is important to pay special attention to signs such as:

~ urinating (or trying to urinate) frequently and in unusual places

~ cats that constantly go in and out of the litter box

~ blood in the urine

ᓚ strong smelling urine

ᓚ vocalizing when urinating

ᓚ frequently licking under the tail.

Report any of these signs to your veterinarian at once. Not only are urinary infections unhealthy, they are very uncomfortable for your pet. It is also important to pay close attention to litter box hygiene and watch for signals that your dog needs to go out to urinate. Some people think their pet may no longer be housebroken, when it may simply be that they cannot get to the appropriate place to urinate quickly enough.

Encouraging Your Pet to Drink More Water

To encourage a healthy urinary system, it is very important to encourage your pet to drink fresh water. Provide plenty of cool fresh water at all times. You may choose to provide several types of drinking stations for your pet through out the house.

ᓚ Many cats and dogs like to drink fresh running water. As a result, there are now several different types of water fountains for pets on the market. (See the Resources section in the back of this book.) Some pets (especially cats) can be suspicious of new things, so make sure you know they are drinking out of the fountain before removing the other water bowls.

ᓚ If at all possible, cater to your pet's wishes for drinking water (except out of the toilet.) Try different types of bowls; some cats and dogs prefer a really wide bowl or have a preference for glass, ceramic, or stainless steel. Many a small dog or cat will appreciate their own glass of water on the night table. (Use caution and/or plastic cups because some animals have been known to *knock over* the glass in the middle of the night!) One client of mine even has two cups on her night table. Both are plastic, but hers has a plastic lid and straw. Now she and her kitty are both happy!

- Another client of mine got her dog to drink more by floating his favorite treats in the water bowl while he was watching. Another client puts a few inches of clean water in her bathroom sink every morning for her cat. Think out of the bowl and provide your pet with plenty of opportunities to get more fluids!

- Adding warm water or broth to your pet's food is another way to get it to consume more liquids. Many veterinarians will recommend feeding more canned food as your pet ages. Remember, with a diabetic pet, it is important to discuss any diet changes with your veterinarian.

To encourage my own cat, Chuck, to drink more water, I add warm water to his canned food, making it very soupy. I then add a topping of Cat-Man-Doo™ dried bonito flakes. He slurps it up every time!

- Low sodium beef, chicken, vegetable broth, or tuna water can be offered to supplement your pet's fresh water. If you are tempted to serve your pet soup, read the list of ingredients carefully, and do not give it to your pet if the soup contains onion powder. Onion powder causes changes to certain blood cells and can cause illness or even death. (Please ask your veterinarian if sodium needs to be restricted.)

- Filtered or spring water is a good idea to use because it may taste fresher and contain fewer particles for the kidneys to process. Distilled water is **not** a good choice, as it may actually flush needed minerals out of the body.

At some point, your veterinarian may recommend giving subcutaneous (SC) injections of saline solution under the skin to support hydration and keep the kidneys flushed. Normal saline solution and lactated ringers solution (LRS) are commonly prescribed types of fluids for in home use. Low potassium levels (hypokalemia) can be an issue with some diabetic pets. For this reason some veterinarians will add potassium to the fluid bag for additional benefit. Vitamin B may also be added to the fluids in case the animal may be deficient in this vitamin (due to poor appetite). Vitamin B can also help stimulate appetite. A trained veterinary technician can show you how to administer the fluids if you chose to do this at home.

As animals age and systems slow down, extra care needs to be taken to keep them safe. Many animals may wander or become lost. Make sure they stay safely contained and away from steps or dangerous places they may wander. Again, make sure your pet has ID on it at all times. Some people choose to have a tag that alerts people to the diabetic condition should someone find the pet. This is an excellent way to ensure that your pet receives the treatment it needs while awaiting its return to you. Containment systems like the Purrfect Fence are an excellent way for pets to continue to enjoy the great outdoors safely. (See Resource section.)

Many behavioral problems may be medical in origin. At any point in your pet's life, especially when being treated for an illness and/or chronic condition, your pet should have a full physical exam and blood work run to rule out a medical condition that may be a cause for behavior issues. It is recommended to do this every six months, as problems in older pets may arise or worsen suddenly. Many undesirable behaviors from our pets are caused by medical problems, being in pain or discomfort. Addressing and treating those needs is very important in keeping your older pet happy and comfortable.

In conclusion, many changes take place in the bodies and minds of our older diabetic pets. As guardians of our beloved furry friends, we can continue to enjoy their company well into their golden years. With good veterinary care, optimal nutrition, and attention to our pet's emotional needs, senior pets with or without diabetes, can live long and comfortable lives.

CHAPTER 16
End of Life Considerations

What you will learn in this chapter:

ᨑ **Where to begin in making an end of life decision**

ᨑ **What are signs of pain**

ᨑ **What is the process of euthanasia**

ᨑ **What is the grieving process**

ᨑ **How pets left behind are affected**

ᨑ **How to cope with your grief**

ᨑ **How to memorialize your pet**

Even with thoughtful and consistent care, the day may come when you are faced with a difficult decision regarding your pet's life. There may be a number of reasons why you are considering euthanasia. It may be the inability to achieve regulation and/or to manage concurrent medical issues in a diabetic pet. It is often difficult to make decisions when your head is telling you one thing and your heart another. That is why it is best to make your decision based on what is best for your pet.

Where to begin in making a decision

Solid information about what you are likely to encounter in the disease process may be helpful in making end-of-life decisions more manageable. Ask your veterinarian for specific information regarding your pet and its medical condition. Discuss with them medical signs to watch for such as seizures, disorientation, difficulty breathing, painful abdomen, etc. It may be helpful to write down a list of signs that your pet may encounter, so you can easily remember what to watch for.

One concept that may help in making a decision is what is my bottom line? This is a guideline by which to measure your pet's quality of life and/or level of deterioration. For some, the bottom line is consistently refusing food, and for others it is difficulty breathing or hiding from and/or avoiding loved ones.

Examples of other situations to help gauge your pet's quality of life:

- Refusal to eat, no matter what is offered.

- Incontinence, especially if the animal is immobile.

- Inability to get up and walk.

- Struggle to get comfortable or inability to get restful sleep.

- Lack of interest/interaction with family members and/or other pets.

Determining if your pet is in pain or feeling unwell can be difficult. Animals by nature try to hide this from us. Some signs to look for are:

- Dilated pupils (a sign of pain).

- Lack of appetite. Some animals may turn their head or move away from food put down near it. Food may make them feel nauseous.

- Vomiting and/or diarrhea.

- Restlessness (a sign of pain).

- Panting or heavy breathing (signs of pain).

- Vocalizing: moaning, growling, or crying (signs of pain or severe discomfort).

- Painful or pinched look to face (a sign of pain or discomfort).

- Hunched up back (a sign of abdominal pain).

- Stumbling and/or falling down.

- Lethargy.

- Not paying attention to detail, sound, or movement in the room.

- Unusual aggressive behavior such as growling or biting people or other pets. This could indicate pain or fear of pain when being touched.

- Although vocalizing can be a sign of pain, current thinking is that it may also be a way that dying animals communicate with us and other animals. By observing your pet's overall condition and attitude, you may be able to differentiate the two.

While no one can (or should) make the decision for you, there are questions to ask yourself that may be helpful in making this difficult decision. In the thoughtful and helpful book 'A Final Act of Caring' by Mary and Herb Montgomery, the authors suggest the following questions.

- Is there a reasonable chance for a cure? For comfort?

- How much additional time might treatment give? What will the quality of that time be?

- Do I have the financial and emotional resources to handle long-term medical care if it is required?

- Will I have the necessary physical and emotional stamina? (Getting up at night, preparing special food, giving shots ....)

- Is the relationship with my pet changing or decreasing in quality as I anticipate this loss?

- How many of my pet's usual activities are still possible? Make a list and review it on a regular basis.

- Is my pet suffering even though physical pain is not evident?

- What do I think my pet would want?

- If I were in my pets place, what would I want?

- What is my personal bottom line-what am I unable to tolerate and/or live with? Write a contract with yourself, knowing you can always renegotiate.

- Project yourself ahead in time and ask "How will I look back and remember this experience?"

It is often very helpful to talk to supportive friends and partners when making this decision. Stay away from people who tell you "It's just a cat or it's just a dog." These people do not understand the love you and your pet share. There are many good books on the subject of pet loss. There are also knowledgeable and understanding people who run pet loss support hotlines and Web sites. Talking to someone may be helpful as you anticipate the loss of your friend. Please check the Resources section of this book for more information.

The process of euthanasia

The word *euthanasia* literally means good death in ancient Greek. Veterinary medicine is fortunate in that we can offer this to our beloved pets and to gently alleviate their suffering. Some people choose to bring their pet into the veterinary office or emergency hospital for this release from suffering, while others opt for an in home euthanasia done by a veterinarian. Whichever way you chose, similar methods are used to ensure you and your pet have as peaceful an experience as possible.

Some people chose to be with their pet during euthanasia, while some cannot. Do not feel badly if you feel you cannot be present. Think of your pet's comfort, will your being upset be upsetting to them?

Another consideration is for families to discuss ahead of time who would like to be present. If small children are to be present, arrange ahead of time to have another adult available or a place the child can go if for any reason they change their mind during the procedure.

You will be asked to sign a form that gives the veterinarian permission to perform this procedure. Even if you have known your veterinarian for years, this is a standard practice because of the nature of the procedure being done and the fact that the injection used is a controlled substance. This means it is a highly regulated substance that is only available to veterinarians with a license to use it.

The billing of this procedure varies. You may ask to pay before the procedure, so you can leave quickly afterward if you need to. Your veterinarian may also agree to bill you. It is always a good idea to ask what the policy is so that things will go as smoothly as possible.

To ensure easy access to a vein, many veterinarians will place an IV catheter (see chapter 13) before the procedure. (Even if your veterinarian doesn't typically do this, you can request it.) Many older animals have problems with circulation. As a result, lack of good blood flow, in combination with disease or illness, can make it hard to find the location of the vein. This can add stress to all involved. Often the technician will ask to take your pet to a treatment area in the hospital to place the IV catheter.

Also, as part of the procedure, many veterinarians will give a mild sedative to ensure the pet does not feel any stress. This also can give the guardian a chance to spend time with the pet in a relaxed state.

When you are ready, the veterinarian will inject the euthanasia solution into your pet's vein. Euthanasia solution is a pentobarbital, a barbiturate that is, in effect an IV (intravenous) anesthetic drug. It is a concentrated form that first causes a deep anesthesia, then breathing to stop, after which the heart stops. It is not uncommon for an animal to have muscle spasms, and it may appear like it is gasping for breath. The diaphragm (a large muscle in the chest) may contract in response to lack of oxygen to the tissues. This is an involuntary response from the body and is not in response to discomfort or pain. Often an animal will urinate and/or defecate after it has passed away. It is a good idea to have an absorbent towel or blanket under your pet during its passing. In the next hour or two an animal's body will cool and the muscles will stiffen.

Veterinary staff can discuss with you the different methods for after-care. Some people chose to do a home burial, while for others either private or group cremation is appropriate. As difficult as it may be, making these arrangements in advance may be easier than having to make them when you are actively grieving.

The grieving process

The process of grieving for a pet is perfectly normal. When people grieve for a loved one, there are several stages of grief that they may experience. These stages have been recognized as denial, sadness, depression, guilt, anger, and finally relief. (These stages are much less predictable in children because of their age and stages of maturity.) Grieving is a completely personal experience that may be different with different people and with different pets. It may last for days or for years. Allowing time to reflect and heal is a great gift you can offer to yourself or someone going through this process.

When other pets are left behind

Whether other family pets were best of friends or merely tolerated each other, the loss of a pet does not go unnoticed by the remaining pets. For this reason, pay close attention to the physical and emotional states of animals left behind. Remaining pets need extra attention and reassurance at this time. The passing of a pet can cause the others to search for and even call out for a missing animal. Some animals may refuse to eat, become depressed and/or antisocial, vocalize more, or become restless when a companion pet is suddenly gone. They may spend more time in places they shared with the pet who is now gone.

It may be helpful for remaining animals to view and have the opportunity to spend time with a deceased pet, although we do not know if animals have the same concept of death that we do.

Occasionally and without solid explanation, some partnered animals will pass away shortly after their companion. They may be especially sensitive to death even with animals they may not have seemed to care for. In my personal experience, my cat Violet, who clearly disliked Alex, curled up in his bed with him before his in-home euthanasia and later remained by his body for about an hour after he passed away, standing as still as a sentry. Several years later when Violet's long-time companion, Sesame, passed away, she went from being a healthy cat to succumbing to multiple health issues in less than six months.

It is very important to consider the feelings of remaining pets in the grieving process. It can be a time of uncertainty for them when a family pet is gone. Household dynamics, routines, and relationships may shift and rearrange with the passing of an animal. This is especially true with dogs because of their social ties with one another. The pack or group may now feel unstable and as a result there may be more competition for attention or resources, and more conflict and/or aggression.

As animals pick up on our feelings easily, part of their depression may be in reaction to that of ours. To help the remaining pets through a difficult time, sticking to routines is vital. Keep feeding schedules, diet, exercise routines, and sleeping arrangements as close to usual as possible. Keeping a routine will help the grieving pet guardian as well as the remaining pets.

Coping with your own grief

Although grieving is an entirely personal experience, there are techniques that may be helpful to those experiencing it. Some things you may try are:

- Acknowledge your feelings and allow yourself the time and space to come to terms with them. If you need to, take a little time away from work or commitments.

- Discuss your feelings with *supportive* friends, family members, or coworkers.

- Write about your feelings. Compose a story or poem about your pet. Record your feelings in a journal.

- Consider joining a pet loss support group. Contact your veterinarian or local humane society to see if there is a group in your area. Some veterinary schools also offer this service.

- Read a book on the subject of pet loss. There are also excellent children's books on this subject.

- Search the Internet for pet loss support groups.

- Memorialize your pet.

Ways to memorialize a beloved pet

♥ Make a scrapbook, artwork, or specially framed picture of your pet.

♥ Hold a celebration of life or memorial service with people who knew and loved your pet. Invite them to bring a can of food or toy to donate to a shelter or rescue group in your pet's honor.

♥ Plant a tree, bush, or flower bed in your yard. If possible, choose a place where your pet spent many happy hours. This offers you a place you can feel especially close to your pet.

♥ Make a donation in your pet's honor to help other less fortunate animals.

♥ Donate a special piece of equipment or item from your local animal shelter's wish list in your pet's honor.

♥ Make a paw print out of clay or clip some fur to keep in a special place.

♥ When the time is right, share your love again with a rescued animal that needs a good home. Everyone will benefit from this.

Although this can be a tremendously sad time, rejoice in the fact that you gave of yourself to a beloved creature that needed your care. In time you may find you are looking forward to beginning a new relationship with an animal. This time period can vary, so give yourself as much time as you need. Don't rush. Whenever you chose, open your heart and you will find another loving companion who will be very fortunate to share its life with you. You'll be so glad you did!

Glossary

Acidosis - an abnormal condition of reduced alkalinity of the blood and tissues. It is marked by sickly sweet breath, nausea and vomiting, and is usually a result of excessive acid production.

Acupuncture - a Chinese practice of inserting fine needles through the skin at specific points in order to cure disease or relieve pain.

Amino acid - types of organic acids that are the chief components of proteins. They are synthesized by living cells or are obtained as essential components of the diet.

Antimicrobial - destroying or inhibiting the growth of microorganisms and especially pathogenic (disease causing) microorganisms.

Biguanides - any of a group of hypoglycemia-inducing drugs (such as metformin) used especially in the treatment of diabetes.

Bilirubin - a reddish-yellow pigment that occurs usually in bile and blood and causes jaundice if accumulated in excess.

Capillary - any of the smallest blood vessels throughout the body.

Casts - a mass of plastic matter formed in cavities of diseased organs (as the kidneys) and discharged from the body.

Cataracts - a clouding of the lens of the eye or its surrounding transparent membrane that obstructs the passage of light.

Cephalic - a large vein of the front leg (dog and cat) lying along the outer edge of the biceps muscle.

Concurrent - occurring at the same time.

Cortisol - a glucocorticoid produced by the adrenal cortex that mediates various metabolic processes, has anti-inflammatory and immunosupressive properties, and whose levels in the blood may become elevated in response to physical or psychological stress.

Cushing's disease - condition resulting from excess amounts of corticosteroid hormones in the body.

Dehydration - an abnormal depletion of body fluids.

Desensitize - to extinguish an emotional response (as of fear, anxiety, or guilt) to stimuli that formerly induced it.

Dextrose - a type of glucose; also called grape sugar.

(Diabetic) Ketoacidosis (DKA) - acidosis accompanied by ketosis.

ECG - electrocardiogram. The tracing made by an electrocardiograph machine that records the changes of electrical potential occurring during the heartbeat. This helps to diagnose abnormalities of heart action.

Electrolyte - any of the ions (sodium, potassium, calcium, or bicarbonate) that in a biological fluid regulate or affect most metabolic processes (as the flow of nutrients into and waste products out of cells).

Epinephrine - the principal blood-pressure-raising hormone secreted by the adrenal medulla. It is also prepared from adrenal extracts or made synthetically and is used medicinally especially as a heart stimulant, as a bronchodilator or to treat glaucoma and life-threatening allergic reactions. It also prolongs the effects of local anesthetics.

Fecal test - a test performed with a fresh stool sample. The test is for intestinal parasites such as hookworms, roundworms, whipworms, coccidia, and giardia. It can also detect an overgrowth of bacteria.

FIV - feline immunodeficiency virus. This virus has been called feline AIDS because of similarities in the two diseases. The AIDS virus affects only humans, and the FIV affects only cats. The virus is primarily spread by free-roaming, intact (not neutered) male cats usually through bite wounds.

FeLV - feline leukemia virus. A common and highly contagious virus that is spread primarily by saliva during cat fights, grooming, or mating. The virus is also spread by blood, urine, and feces.

Fight or flight response - When animals perceive a significant threat, their bodies get ready either for a fight with the threat or a flight from the threat. A number of physiological changes take place in the body to prepare for this.

Gauge - the diameter of a slender object (as a hypodermic needle).

Glucagon - a protein hormone that is produced especially by the pancreatic islets of Langerhans and that promotes an increase in the sugar content of the blood by increasing the rate of breakdown of glycogen in the liver.

Glucocorticoids - any of a group of corticosteroids (as cortisol or dexamethasone) that are involved especially in carbohydrate, protein, and fat metabolism, that are anti-inflammatory and immunosuppressive, and that are used widely in medicine (as in the alleviation of the signs of rheumatoid arthritis).

Glucose - the sweet colorless soluble substance that occurs widely in nature and is the usual form in which carbohydrates are used by animals.

Glucosuria - the presence in the urine of abnormal amounts of sugar.

Glycemic Indices (or index) - a numerical scale used to indicate how fast and how high a specific food can raise blood glucose levels. A food with a low GI will cause a moderate rise in blood glucose, while a food with a high GI may cause blood glucose levels to increase sharply.

Heparin - an acid ester that occurs especially in the liver and lungs, and that prolongs the clotting time of blood by preventing the formation of fibrin.

Hormones - a product of living cells that circulates in body fluids (as blood) and produces a specific often stimulatory effect on the activity of cells usually remote from its point of origin.

Hyperglycemia - an excess of sugar in the blood.

Hyperthyroidism - excessive functional activity of the thyroid gland; the resulting condition marked especially by increased metabolic rate, enlargement of the thyroid gland, rapid heart rate, and high blood pressure .

Hypoglycemia - abnormal decrease of sugar in the blood.

Hypothyroidism - deficient activity of the thyroid gland; also a resulting bodily condition characterized by lowered metabolic rate and general loss of vigor.

Immune Mediated - the immune system attacking the body.

Insulin - a protein hormone that is secreted by the beta cells of the islets of Langerhans in the pancreas that is essential for the metabolism of carbohydrates, lipids, and proteins. It also regulates blood sugar levels by facilitating the uptake of glucose into tissues and reduces the release of glucose from the liver.

Insulin Resistance - reduced sensitivity to insulin by the body's insulin-dependent processes that result in lowered activity of these processes or an increase in insulin production or both.

Intravenous - situated within, performed within, occurring within, or administered by entering a vein.

Ketonemia -a condition marked by an abnormal increase of ketone bodies in the circulating blood.

Ketones - ketones are intermediate products of fat metabolism.

Ketonuria - the presence of excess ketone bodies in the urine in conditions such as diabetes mellitus.

Ketosis - an abnormal increase of ketone bodies in the body in conditions such as uncontrolled diabetes mellitus.

Metabolism - the chemical changes in living cells by which energy is provided for vital processes and activities and new material is assimilated.

Neuropathy - an abnormal and usually degenerative state of the nervous system or nerves; also a systemic condition that stems from a neuropathy.

Obligate Carnivore - animals that must eat meat in order to thrive.

Omnivore - an animal that feeds on both animal and vegetable substances.

Otoscope - an instrument fitted with lighting and magnifying lens systems and used to facilitate visual examination of the ear canal and eardrum.

Pancreas - a large gland that secretes digestive enzymes and the hormones insulin and glucagon.

Pancreatitis - inflammation of the pancreas.

pH- a measure of acidity and alkalinity of a solution that is a number on a scale on which a value of seven represents neutrality and lower numbers indicate increasing acidity and higher numbers increasing alkalinity.

Plantigrade - walking on the sole with the heel touching the ground.

Platelets - a minute colorless disk like body of mammalian blood that is derived from fragments of cytoplasm. It is released from the bone marrow into the blood, and assists in clotting.

Progesterone - a female steroid sex hormone that is secreted to prepare the endometrium for implantation and later by the placenta during pregnancy to prevent rejection of the developing embryo or fetus.

Seizure - the physical manifestations (as convulsions, sensory disturbances, or loss of consciousness) resulting from abnormal electrical discharges in the brain; also an abnormal electrical discharge in the brain.

Specific Gravity - the ratio of the density of a substance to the density of some substance (as pure water) taken as a standard when both densities are obtained by weighing in air.

Superfamily - a category of taxonomic classification between a family and an order or a suborder.

Taxonomically - orderly classification of plants and animals according to their presumed natural relationships.

Unregulated Diabetes - diabetes that is not under control.

Vein - any of the tubular branching vessels that carry blood from the capillaries toward the heart.

Resources

Information on what is diabetes

- **American College of Veterinary Internal Medicine**
  Information on treating diabetes in pets
  http://www.acvim.org/websites/acvim/index.php?p=210

- **Feline Diabetes** - Information on treating diabetes in cats
  www.FelineDiabetes.com

- **Pet Diabetes Wiki** - Over 400 articles and 100 case studies.
  Affiliated with felinediabetes.com
  www.petdiabetes.wikia.com

- **Pets With Diabetes**
  Providing educational information, Internet resources, personal
  experiences, and support for owners of diabetic pets
  http://www.caninediabetes.org/pdorg/

- **Sugarpet.net** - Information on treating diabetes in cats
  www.sugarpet.net

Information on financing options

- **CareCredit®** – CareCredit is a personal line of credit for healthcare
  treatments, for people and pets. This will be very convenient in
  emergency situations.
  (866) 893-7864
  www.carecredit.com

- **Chase Health Advantage** – Flexible financing for health care, including veterinary care.
  (888) 519-6111
  www.chasehealthadvance.com

- **Citi® Health Card** – Flexible financing for health care, including veterinary care.
  (866) 832-8762
  www.healthcard.citcards.com

- **Wells Fargo Health Advantage** – Patient payment plan solutions, including veterinary care.
  (877) 231-0294
  www.financial.wellsfargo.com

Information on treatment options

- **The Academy of Veterinary Homeopathy** – Information on homeopathy, including how to find names of veterinarians who practice homeopathy.
  www.theavh.org
  (305) 652-1590

- **American Holistic Veterinary Medical Association** - AHVMA – Information on holistic veterinary medicine, including how to find a holistic veterinarian in your area.
  www.ahvma.org
  (410) 569-0795

- **Animal Apawthecary Herbs** **(Sold through Animal Essentials)**
  (406) 821-4090
  www.animalessentials.com

- **Dr. Goodpet** – Natural pet pharmacy for dogs and cats. Sells nutritional supplements, homeopathic remedies, etc.
  www.goodpet.com
  (800) 222-9932

- **HomeoPet** – Information and distribution of homeopathic remedies for animals
  www.homeopet.com
  (800) 434-0449

- **International Veterinary Acupuncture Society** – Information on veterinary acupuncture, including information on how to find a veterinarian that practices acupuncture.
  www.ivas.org
  (303) 449-7936

- **Standard Process** – Nutritional supplements sold through health care professionals.
  www.standardprocess.com
  (800) 848-5061

Information on Diet

- **Champion Pet Foods** – Makers of Orijen pet foods. Orijen dry and canned foods are grain free.
  www.championpetfoods.com
  (877) 939-0006

- **4 Paws Homemade Natural Food** – Raw food diets for cats and dogs. Custom diets and local delivery available.
  Vanda Glaspey, Eugene OR
  (541) 345-5818
  natural4paws@aol.com

- **Feeding Your Cat: Know the Basics of Feline Nutrition** – Large amount of information on feline nutrition. Written by Lisa A. Pierson, DVM
  www.catinfo.com

- **Merrick Pet Care** – Makers of Merrick pet foods, including Before Grain. Before Grain canned and dry foods are grain free.
  www.merrickpetcare.com
  (800) 664-7387

- **Pet Togethers** – Understanding homemade diets and the pros and cons of a raw food (BARF) diets. Written by Shawn Messonnier, DVM
www.pettogethers.com/powerreports/understandinghome-madediet.aspx

- **PHD** – Pet Healthy Diet - Raw food diet for cats and dogs – Organic whenever possible, human grade ingredients, no chemicals or artificial additives. Diabetic diets and delivery available.
JP Persyn, Eugene, OR
(541)935-3082

- **Rad Cat™** – Premium Raw Food for Cats. Organic, hormone and antibiotic free, using free-range or pasture-raised meat. Website includes great information including transitioning your cat to raw food.
(503) 736-4649
www.radfood.com

- **Real Food Toppers** – Pure dehydrated chicken breast, wild salmon, beef liver and beef sirloin. Can be used as treats or food toppers to encourage eating. Excellent for diabetic pets.
(866) 807-7335
www.completenaturalnutrition.com

- **Reading a Pet Food Label**
www.specialneedspets.org/nutrition.htm

- **WildSide Salmon** - All natural products for cats and dogs. Excellent treats for diabetic pets.
www.wildsidesalmon.com
(206) 722-FISH

Information on toys and exercise

- **Cat Fence-In** – Cat Containment System. Keeps cats safe in your backyard and keeps other cats out.
  (888) 738-9099
  www.catfencein.com

- **Go-Cat Toys** – Quality interactive toys handcrafted in the USA. Maker of Da-Bird, Da Bee, and the fantastic Cat Catcher.
  (517) 543-7519
  www.go-cat.com

- **Habitat Haven** – Safe, healthy Habitats for Pets. Makers of products for cats, dogs and birds, including outdoor enclosures.
  (416) 466-8930\
  www.habitahaven.com

- **Kittywalk® Systems, Inc.** - Kittywalk designs and sells indoor and outdoor use pet products that are designed to keep your favorite friend safe, but have fun doing it.
  (877) 548-8905
  www.kittywalk.com

- **Ohio State University College of Veterinary Medicine – Indoor Cat Initiative**
  Information for improving the lives of indoor cats
  www.veterinarian.ohio-state.edu/indoorcat.htm

- **Purrfect Fence** - Cat Fencing system that safely keeps cats within a designated area. Excellent way for cats to get exercise and fresh air safely.
  www.PurrfectFence.com
  (888) 280- 4066

- **Smart Cat Toys** -Makers of the peek a prize, peek and play toy box and other smart products for smart cats.
  (866)-31SMART (317-6278)
  www.esmartcat.com

Information on supplies

- **Abbott Laboratories** – Manufacturer of Alpha Trak glucometers for cats and dogs
(847) 937-6100
www.abbott.com

- **Animal Diabetes Management** – Manufacturer of GlucoPet glucometer
(866) 391-9436
www.animaldiabetes.com

- **Bayer** - Manufacturer of glucometers including Ascensia Contour
(800) 348-8100
www.bayerdiabetes.com

- **Bach® Flower Remedies** – Makers of Rescue Remedy and 38 flower remedies
(800) 214- 2850
www.bachflower.com

- **BD** - Diabetic supplies and information
www.bddiabetes.com
(201) 847-6800

- **Flower Essence Society** – Flower Essences
(800) 736-9222
www.flowersociety.org

- **Hocks.com** - Diabetic supplies
www.hocks.com
(800) 898-8570

- **LifeScan** – Manufacturer of glucometers including One Touch Ultra
(800) 227-8862
www.ifescan.com

- **Ulti-Med Inc.** – Manufacturer of iPet™ glucometer
  (877) 858-4633
  www.vetrxsupply.com

- **Zöe** - Needle free insulin jet
  www.zoepetjet.com
  (866) 235-2673

Information on home testing procedures

- **Understanding Home Blood Glucose Meters** – Detailed information on blood glucose meters, including recommendations
  www.caninediabetes.org/pdorg/bgmeterconcepts.htm

Information on blood glucose testing at home

- **The Breeze Litter System**
  www.breezeforcats.com

- **Hometesting Harry**
  www.sugarcats.net
  www.sugarcats.net/sites/harry/bgtest.htm

- **Dr. Lisa's Hometesting Information**
  www.catinfo.org
  www.catinfo.org/felinediabetes.htm#In-Home_Blood_Glucose_Monitoring

- **Feline Diabetes Message Board Page**
  www.felinediabetes.com
  www.felinediabetes.com/bg-test

- **The Smart Cat Box** – User and ecologically friendly cat box. Doubles as a urine collection system.
  (541) 563-4443
  www.smartcatbox.com

☙ **Sugarcat Hometesting Primer**
www.gorbzilla.com
www.gorbzilla.com/Gorb%27s%20home%20testing%20primer.htm

Information on traveling and your diabetic pet

☙ **FasTags®** - The original shrinking ID tag you make at home for you dog or cat.
(866) 412-6860
www.fastags.com

☙ **HomeAgain** – All inclusive pet recovery and protection service, using microchip technology.
Available through your veterinarian.
(888) -HOMEAGAIN (466-3242)
www.homeagain.com

☙ **idtag.com** – Identification system includes online access to personal pet & owner profile, instant lost pet alerts to shelters and 24-hour emergency customer support.
(866) 60-FOUND
www.idtag.com

☙ **Microchip ID** – makers of Avid (American Veterinary Identification Device) microchips. Also available registration in PETtrac Recovery Network, global 24 hour database used by shelters and anyone finding a lost pet.
Available through your veterinarian, shelter, etc.
www.Microchipsystems.com

☙ **National Association of Professional Pet Sitters** - Website includes information including how to locate a pet sitter.
(800) 296-PETS
www.petsitters.org

☙ **Pet Care Services Association** – Website offers information including how to locate a pet care facility.
(877) 570-7788
www.petcareservices.org

- **Pet Sitters International** – Website includes information including how to locate a pet sitter.
(336) 983-9222
www.petsit.com

Information on senior pets

- **Drinkwell Pet Fountain (Veterinary Ventures)** Water fountains for cats and dogs that encourage drinking.
(866) 322-2530
www.petfountains.com

- **Fat Cat Creations** – Litterbox Containment Furniture. Also works great for concealing food bowls, dogs can't get to the cat's food. Easier than climbing up to the counter for elderly and diabetic cats.
(604) 756-0267
www.bigfatkittycat.com

- **Precious Cat Litters** – Dr. Elsey's Litterbox Solutions. Manufacturer of the only litter designed for cats that do not consistently use their litter box. Every bag has a free Dr. Elsey solutions booklet inside giving you answers to solve your cats litter box aversion.
(877) 311-2287
www.preciouscat.com

- **Ramp4Paws®** - Roll out, roll up dog ramp.
(888) 654-7297
www.ramp4paws.com

- **SeniorPetProducts.com** Distributor of products for senior pets. Website includes articles, senior pet blog and information.
(800) 523-7979
www.seniorpetproducts.com

Information on end of life considerations

- **Angel ashes** – Pet urns
(800) 839-4604
www.angelashes.com

☙ **Association for Pet Loss and Bereavement** – Offers many good web pages, including information on euthanasia, aftercare, children and loss, etc.
(718) 382-0690
www.aplb.com

☙ **Cornell University College of Veterinary Medicine**-Offers pet loss support hotline, support group and resources.
(607) 253-3932
www.veterinarian.cornell.edu/org/petloss/

☙ **Mary and Herb Montgomery** – Authors of Good Bye My Friend: Grieving the Loss of a Pet, A Final Act of Caring: Ending the Life of an Animal Friend and Your Aging Pet: Making the Senior Years Healthy and Rewarding. Beautifully written and illustrated books.
Montgomery Press
PO Box 24124, Minneapolis, MN 55424
(952) 928-0826

☙ **Nikki Hospice Foundation for Pets** – Veterinary Hospice Care
www.pethospice.org
(707) 557-8595

☙ **Petloss.com** – Compassionate website for pet lovers who are grieving. Offers support, advice, etc.
www.petloss.com

☙ **Rainbow Bridge Urns** – Pet memorialization items including urns, plaques, markers and keepsake jewelry.
(877) 268-2912
www.rainbowbridgeurns.com

☙ **Spirits in Transition** – Options in end of life care for animal companions
www.spiritsintransition.com

General Information:

∾ **Animal Wellness Magazine** – Health magazine for cats and dogs
www.animalwellnessmagazine.com

∾ **ASPCA Animal Poison Control Center** – Resource for animal
poison related emergencies, 24/7, 365 days a year. A $60 consul-
tation fee may be applied to your credit card.
(888) 426-4435
www.aspca.org

∾ **PetEdge** - Supplier of pet supplies and products
(800) 698-9062
www.petedge.com

∾ **Petfinder** – Find your next best friend online. Petfinder is the
temporary home of 297,662 adoptable pets from 12,250 adop-
tion groups.
www.petfinder.

∾ **Lost Pets** – Search and rescue for lost pets. Information on the
behavior of lost pets and how to find them.
www.lostapet.org

∾ **MMilani.com** – Integrating health, behavior, and the human
animal bond
www.mmilani.com

∾ **2ⁿᵈ Chance for Pets** – A non-profit organization devoted to protecting beloved animal companions so they will receive lifetime
care even if they are orphaned by their owners death or disability.
(408) 871-1133
www.2ndchance4pets.org

∾ **Special Needs Pets** – Resources, Information and Support
www.specialneedspets.org